LOVE SONGS

of the

ZOMBIE

To humanity at the Dawn of a New Millennium

To justify the ways of God to people
On Philosophy, Religion, Science, and Art

RONALD STEPHENS

MINDSTIR MEDIA

Published by MindStir Media, LLC
45 Lafayette Rd | Suite 181| North Hampton, NH 03862 | USA
1.800.767.0531 | www.mindstirmedia.com

Printed in the United States of America.
ISBN-13: 978-1-961532-94-6

Table of Contents

Dedication

Montauk Point

It was 1995 and my family had just moved from the Midwest to Connecticut. The kids had never seen the ocean and we were eager to find a beach to enjoy, so we crossed over to Long Island and set out along the southeastern shore facing the wide-open Atlantic Ocean. It was a spectacular weekend day and, unfortunately, every beach was filled, with no parking and no entry, so we just kept on going. Long Island is a very long island, and every beach was full up all the way until we reached the very tip of the island, Montauk Point, with ocean all around us on all three sides. For some reason, the beautiful beach here was almost completely empty, but the day was almost over so we hurried out of the car and into the water before the last minutes of sunlight were gone. We felt very lucky to have found this beach just in time.

We didn't get very far out from shore before we were caught up in a surprising riptide. It was so powerful that we were washed a bit further out before we knew what had hit us. As each tremendous wave came in, we were all swept off our feet, and as each wave receded, we could again touch the bottom with our feet, but we were pulled back and knocked down again. I didn't know anything about how to deal with riptides. I now know that the best thing to do is to first try to move perpendicular to the tide (parallel to the shore) in order to get out of the most vicious part of the current, and only then work towards the shore. But at the time, my only strategy was to try to head straight for shore as quickly as possible. This, however, pitted us against the most powerful strength of the riptide.

My three daughters and my wife were completely unable to remain standing or make any progress at all against the tide. I tried to help them one at a time, as quicky as I could, because I couldn't possibly help them all at the same time. I would throw each of my daughters forward, then go on to the next, and finally frantically push or pull my wife forward. But this meant that each of them was knocked down and underwater as soon as I was helping the others. Each of them frantically screamed at me to not abandon them, but I had to divide my efforts amongst all four. It appeared that we would die. I prayed fervently and constantly, for there are no atheists in foxholes. It was unbelievable that such a simple mistake and situation could cost us our lives, but the reality of the situation was what it was. I also frantically reviewed in my mind the possibility that some of the family might make it, but not all. I doubted if I could help save all four, but how could I live with myself if some survived but not all made it out alive? It would be as if I had decided which ones would live. It was the most terrifying thing I could ever imagine, but all I could do was to expend maximum effort to try to move each of them forward to the shore, even as I heard the horrified cries each time, as I moved on to the next one to help. Meanwhile, I also was being knocked down with each wave cycle.

Finally, miraculously, somehow we reached the shore. It had been almost beyond my hopes and expectations that we would be able to do so, but we did. However, the "shore" that we reached was a big unclimbable cliff, quite a bit higher than my head or my reach, even when I managed to stand up against the surging surf. We had been washed down shore, and in that direction the beach gradually turned into a cliff. There was no way we could move along the shore (believe me, I tried) back in the direction in which the cliff got smaller, because the over-powering tide was washing us in the other direction, in which the cliff got even higher. The bitter irony was we were going to die, even after having fought back to the shore against all odds.

But then, a strong right arm reached down from atop the cliff to help us, and grabbed the hand of each family member, one at a time, and lifted them to safety. I could not see the person, just the strong arm reaching down to save us. No words were spoken. Lastly, he pulled me to safety atop the cliff. As soon as I saw my family safe, I turned around to profusely thank him, the man who saved us, but he was nowhere to be found. There was no sign that he had ever been there, and I couldn't believe or understand what had happened. I was dumbfounded, speechless, and I didn't know what to make of it at all. But mostly I was just too grateful and happy to be safe and sound with my family, without any energy left to think about how it had all transpired.

After all, I was not a prophet or a scholar, nor the son of a prophet or a scholar, just a very simple man who was in completely over his head, so at the time I just went on with my life. But as I write this dedication in the Year of our Lord 2022, I look back and I take it to mean that God is alive and takes a strong hand in the affairs of human beings.

Thank God, and thank the angel who saved us on that fateful day in 1995.

Foreword

Thus Spake Zarathustra

Sometimes an ancient prophet pops up like a zombie from the dead. Nietzsche invoked Zarathustra (the founder of Zoroastrianism) from the grave in order to put new words in his mouth, supporting Nietzsche's theses that "God is Dead" and that people should move "Beyond Good and Evil" and do whatever their own individual "Will to Power" prompts them to do. Nietzsche saw religious morality as a slave mentality and urged people to become Supermen (Ubermensch). Nietzsche was brilliant but his philosophy was nihilistic and misguided, and he misappropriated Zarathustra to support positions diametrically opposite to Zoroastrianism.

Zarathustra taught that there is a perpetual war between good and evil, with good and evil being very real spiritual realities, and emphasized the importance of the threefold path of "Good Thoughts, Good Words, and Good Deeds". The primary choice of each person is between Good and Evil. As Bob Dylan sings "You gotta serve somebody, it may be the devil, or it may be the Lord, but you gotta serve somebody". To serve implies more than just following the rules, but to love and cherish the good. Jesus taught us that just following external rules is not enough, it's what's in the heart that matters more. One should follow the rules for the right reasons, and understand and focus on what's behind the rules, the reasons for the rules, the underlying meaning. Ultimately, one should choose good over evil because of love and appreciation for the good rather than fear of punishment for doing evil.

Many great prophets have taught us about the difference between Good and Evil, and how to live a good life. Their specific dogmas and doctrines may fade, but their teachings about how to live a good life do not fade. But it goes beyond that. Each person should also seek to find their role in life, to discern what is the doable good that they alone can do best. God gives people the opportunity to participate in creation, the unfolding of the underlying reality and the fulfillment of purpose.

Introduction

It is fashionable these days to describe the world deductively, from the top down, coming from a strong belief in secular materialism; hypothesizing a multiverse with an infinite number of universes and an infinite amount of time, in which everything that can exist does exist; and deducing that the universe is purposeless, godless, meaningless, and indifferent to human life. Everything is an accident.

But this theory of everything can be a theory of nothing, if the starting assumptions and theories are incorrect.

I prefer to start from the bottom up, grounded in what's closest to us as conscious human beings, our actual lived experiences, both now and as recorded from the past, and by using inductive reasoning to tease out and discern the higher-level principles and meanings.

So, this book is not a mere collection of short pieces, but rather a unified whole made up of short vignettes, each of which is based on real human experience. Distilled over a period of more than fifty years (from the late 1960s to 2023), it is the first book published by the author.

The book reflects a life-long concern with, and contemplation of, the mysteries and paradoxes of human existence. Because it explores the boundary between the knowable and the unknowable, it uses a variety of forms and styles of expression including both verse and prose. Some may be offended in that large portions of the book use verse, which may be viewed as obsolete and obtuse. This is not done for merely stylistic reasons, but rather in order to compress the information into the most compact, efficient, and effective work of communication possible. Please note that more than half the book is in prose.

Some major influences on the work come from three sources: the King James Bible, translations of classical Chinese poetry into English, and the vast and fabulous treasury of poetry written in the English language. Other influences include the Greek and Latin classics, the books of Teilhard de Chardin, Frank J. Tipler, Cervantes, and Dostoevsky, as well as twentieth century popular song, especially that of Bob Dylan.

While the order of presentation has been carefully chosen, with a coherent thread running from beginning to end, it does not have to be read in that order. After all, it was not written in that order. You are encouraged to read and experience it in any way in which the spirit moves you, and in fact it is hoped that you will come back again and again to parts of it.

The book is made up of four parts. "New Psalms" are lyrical poems that explore the existential questions of human life and are similar to and somewhat inspired by the Book of Psalms in the Bible. They are concerned with the core philosophical questions that are at the heart of human life.

"Analects" are short poems and aphorisms in the tradition of such poems from classical Chinese literature, as read in translation into English. These poems delve into the more personal and intimate aspects of ordinary life, often leading to thoughts and emotions that are anything but ordinary. If you are short on time or attention, read these first. Not just bits and pieces, each verse focuses intently on an essential quintessence of reality.

"Manifesto" is similar to "New Psalms," but the poems are more assertive and aggressive, looking into the same themes but with a sharper edge to them.

"Meditations" are prose pieces including prose poems, prayers, parables, and essays. These explore similar issues to those explored in "New Psalms", but with the kind of added depth, clarity, and straightforwardness facilitated by using prose. To those who abhor poetry, try this section first!

Again, this is not a mere collection of articles; rather, in order to respect the reader's time, it is a highly curated, collated, edited, and condensed work of communication.

New Psalms

晨 音

Ur Human

Born here against our will, so soon to die,
And to what purpose, what's the reason why?
Can't stop the clock, no time to plan or chart,`
We're done before we find a place to start.

After a while it's all just one big blur,
Only thing certain, we know nothing for sure.
Experimental trip from womb to tomb,
Big bang or black hole, to us it's all doom.

Diverse religions, unforgiven sins,
Influences of forces beyond our ken;
Unclean our past, unforeseen our future,
Bathed in blood, red in claw our nature.

And yet I choose to see an unknown god,
A reason for the path ancestors trod.
I sing to purpose, pure and unbegotten,
Of suffering messiahs long forgotten.

I swear to the stars, for humankind's sake,
Be there no meaning, then meaning we'll make.
Each rock, each atom, will work for the good,
As quantum fields, and tears, are understood.

I come from a long line of survivors,
My cells lead sentient lives and so do yours.
Y-chromosomes all know their fathers well,
And mitochondria their mothers tell.

Porous membranes selectively embrace reality,
The self is small but not our whole society,
Nietzsche is dead but not our whole community,
All nature is the future of humanity.

Reason To Believe

Existence speaks:

So everything that is, evolved from nothing,
And we ourselves, like Homo Floresiensis,
Evolved from brainless little creatures
By merest chance, yes, that is the consensus.

If God exists, He sure does keep it secret,
Withholding all the real important things.
He keeps us in the dark, without a clue
To seek and search for what the future brings.

Yes, humankind is quite ridiculous,
We share our flesh and genes with pigs,
We can't control our passions nor our natures,
We dress them up with lipstick and with wigs.

For stuff, the universe, and us are chance;
But God must have some uses of His own,
And since he left us in a world gone wrong,
What do our pain and agony atone?

Gnosis speaks:

If all were known at once, right from the start,
And if our home were perfect in the stars,
If all were certain and we knew the ends,
Our limits would be lower than they are.

God keeps us in the dark, so when we see,
Our eyes are dazzled by the blazing light;
He saves celestial music 'till the end,
So hearing it is maximum delight.

But most surprising is that we can know,
How strange that dust can reason and discern?
A miracle of miracles for sure
That we can cipher, calculate, and learn.

And whether God is hidden or a myth,
We can't survive a life without a hope;
If it be true or it be false, without
A reason to believe we cannot cope.

Against all odds, we face what fate may bring,
We sacrifice our lives, our thoughts, our honor,
Devise and fashion plans, make peace with death,
Create the virtues, give our blood for others.

So God, by hiding, gave us tough love's chance;
To make a world of meaning all our own,
To earn the ecstasies of art sublime,
Not just enjoy, at ease, what we were shown.

So sometimes nothing's a pretty cool hand,
Like in Ben Hur when Charlton Heston
Refused to let his Roman master drown:
The reasons to believe? Belief and Reason.

Ground Zero

We went there often, and on a clear day
We saw Bear Mountain fifty miles away,
We looked at planes eye-level or below,
Had fun and pizza, it was quite a show.

Defined now by its absence, all is changed,
Our lives, our world, they've been re-arranged,
There now are holes where once the towers stood,
Gigantic fountains, museums, and a wood.

It's like when Nietzsche saw infinity,
He said that God is dead; in reality
He saw a hole where once was Deity;
Gödel and he both found insanity.

I sort of think it's like that with our souls,
We die and leave our information holes
Behind; connections broken on the shoals
Of unmet dreams and unfulfilled life's goals.

An information hole can never die,
It twists and turns as ages roll on by,
But never is erased completely 'cause
You just rewind the clock of nature's laws.

What tore time's fabric hurt us to the core,
It left behind a wound that's bloody sore;
We're less now than we were yet strangely more
For now we've been what we but were before.

Advice to a Young Person

Hallelujah! Praise the Lord and all his minions
I've been to the mountaintop and seen the other side
No matter what's ailing you, listen to my story
Because there's a kind of poetic justice that abides.

When I was just about knee-high to a pup
I bought the Kool-Aid and drank it up
But somewhere about my 40th year
I began to see by the light of a different day.

Because you only get one chance at life
You better inhale it and like it a lot
No matter what kind of crap is going down
You only get one life and no second go 'round.

So learn about how to tell right from wrong
And when to bend a bit just to get along
Discern and develop a sense of timing
How to go with the flow and follow big Mo'.

Then find your bliss and stick with it
And learn how to like the bad stuff too
Especially learn how to like the bad stuff
'Cause you'll be seeing plenty of that for sure.

But when your days are dark
And your nights are long
When pain is really all you feel
'Cause life's got you by the throat
And you're so nauseous you can't even throw up

Right then and there and only then
You can conquer life's banality and death's finality
By seeing the justice in the glory that abides.

The birds singing in tune
Dogs loving life and their masters
Babies full of promise being born
Old folks' wisdom in solitude
The sky so full of stars, and moonlit nights
The gentle breeze that blows as evening falls

So put it all on the line and let it ride
Because there's a kind of poetic justice that abides.

Recursion of the Centaur

Luxurious, growing, living,
forest of my dreams.

Yet the forest was not me; I stood on a big Rock
Outcropping on the edge of a
Dark, beautiful, and dangerous stream.

Then, I took my mind
and left it on the Rock
while I crossed, without it, the sparkling stream.

Then stood on a smaller rock
Perched precariously above
The other edge of the stream.

Looking back, I saw a good, healthy fish
In the stream, looking up at me
Big eyes focused on me,
Lips moving, tail wagging below,
A good fish with scales.

Aware that the fish was not me
and that the mind perched across the stream on the big high Rock
Was not me either.

I turned and ran carefully into the verdant woods

But the woods were not me

Nor was the fish

Nor was the mind

Who am I?
What am I?

Aware that folks have
made idols of wood and stone, of beast and bird,
but being neither fish nor fowl,
I was careful not to
worship any of these.

Neither, especially, did I worship my mind
Perched opposite on the Rock,
Aware that in this day and age
We meld our images in the very mind of man.

The Holy Spirit is Wholly Spirit

In the Beginning, God conceived a Cosmos
So perfect and complex, so simple and divine
But lacking any substance firm and physical.
So God exhaled the very breath of Life

A measuring spirit by spirit measured
An animating angel mixed with Chaos
Breath quickened Cosmos with the gift of Life
Made physical within the Mind of God.

But only step by step, time's tiny footsteps
Realized conceived Cosmos as a World
Of flesh and blood, of stick and stone and space
Made Real by God via His Holy Ghost.

So mind came first, the consciousness of God
And then a matrix of lattice network
But only breath by breath of Holy Ghost
Do we partake communion with His consciousness.

So subtle is the spirit of the Lord
It goeth where it listeth like the wind
We feel it in our minds but doubt its worth
Because it lacks the substance of real earth.

Can spirit move a mountain from its place?
Can ghost make men stand firm against a sword?
Does spirit buy our bread and feed our bodies?
Does breath have value like a dollar's clout?

And yet when on my couch I lie at rest
And contemplate the cosmos and my fate
A still small voice commands me to rehearse
The worth of my own soul and inner source.

Without a spirit, a cosmos isn't real
Without a mind, time is an illusion
Without a consciousness all is dead
My inner voice is really all there is.

The Holy Spirit is pure and clean
It washes over me like pleasant rain
I'm centered and I'm home and free at last
At joy in communion with utmost being.

No need to think what I will say or do
For life and life more abundantly
Pours forth like precious oil from inner springs
No pressure to perform, but simply be.

You can't touch it but you can feel it
You can't define it but you can be it
You can't prove it but you can move with it
The weirdness of destiny is Holy Spirit.

My consciousness so loves the Holy Spirit
I long to always move more nigh and near it
To listen for its voice so I can hear it
To sing its praises, revel, and revere it.

The Holy Spirit is Wholly Spirit
We are safe and sound when we are near it
It's in our soul, no need to fear it
The very breath of Life is Wholly Spirit.

Ouroboros

I am a Zombie, possessed by the dead
Who speak to me softly words best left unsaid,
Directing my thoughts to the darkest of dooms
Where at the gates of hell, salvation looms...

My heart and my lungs are like two aching holes
Pumping life's blood into their hallowed souls,
The blood connecting womb of all mankind,
If there's an answer then it's there to find.

Oh Lord above, I pray have ears to hear
When I was young you always were so near,
I thirst to know what I shall die to be
My God, My God, why have you forsaken me?

Oh soul! Go dig a well so deep in the ground
It taps the spring where living waters abound,
Waters so purified by living loam
They fertilize fresh shoots from old rhizome.

Our gods are dead but they haunt our marrow
Pointing the way to a new tomorrow,
Invoking a vision of paradise
And paying the price with their sacrifice.

If life's to be worth living, we must dream
And dreaming, we must wake, and dreams redeem:
Our gods must germinate and be reborn
Transfigured, and of superstition shorn.

The Cave

The mountain man can stand more pain than most,
He lives much closer to the Holy Ghost.
Rough-hewn survivor and by tempest tossed,
He's proud and free but knows what freedom costs.

On sunny days, the storm lurks close behind,
As lazy rivers down the canyon wind.
The wise man scans the cliffs for shelter rock,
To hole up from the fury of the shock.

So seek a cave that's deep and dark and precious,
That when the storm clouds come will be most gracious;
Where safe as night and hidden underground,
The secrets of the heart are often found.

Inside the cave, you'll find a wondrous sight,
Flickering moments shown by candlelight.
An angel, purple gown and golden crown,
Wearing a warm wool shawl all wrapped around

Her shoulders and her luminescent wings
Shine bright; the rubies in her silver rings
Sparkle; she stills your soul and softly sings
Of peace; a message brought to earth for kings.

The Multiverse

The roiling water fills the inlet beach,
The gulls enjoy the misty ocean's reach,
The bounteous beauty is for all to share,
But then of course there is no meaning there.

It is a grand and awesome multiverse,
We watch two qubits dance and dress rehearse,
Then kiss and cohere into an entangled pair,
But then of course there is no meaning there.

They say it takes observance to commit,
Qubits to defined and final bits,
Old Heisenberg was certain it was fair,
But then of course there is no meaning there.

The nothingness they call the quantum foam,
Produces all that is, such fertile loam,
Each possibility will find a home,
In nature's tome; so that even this poem

Was sure to be written, for you to share,
But then of course there is no meaning there.

Creek Bank Cacophony

Oh, what a weird and wicked world is this
A world gone wrong, a cold insipid song
Sung by wild dogs in heated carnal bliss
Who eat their vomit, 'fore they die 'ere long.

We suck the venom from a serpent's tooth
We fight for fame and glory while we cuss
Our fates, our uselessness, our search for truth
Infinite pain, and then a quietus.

But at the river's edge a flower grows
Midst chaos and mud, water, fish and blood
Where worm eats worm, a fleeting beauty shows
Forth startling, vivid colors in the flood.

In this old vale of woe, of stress and strife
We dream a paradise, eternal life.

Spiritus Mundi

From the deep shadows I come to the Magdala
From the sacred corridors of the Kabbala,

I feel communion with the grass, trees, and all animals
As pulsing energy flows from life's inner core
Aware of sacred oil that pours, my cup brimmeth o'er
Partaking of a common living metaphor
I feel that this is what life and living's worth is for
A common destiny, a true blood imaginal.

There is also a transformation algebra
Leading to the habitat of Mount Moriah,

Our next waystation as we tread the path of love
Where communion is of a different order
And there is an underlying number
Approached without the need of slumber
As our senses we unencumber
This is the pervasive matrix from above.

Then on to alpha, beta, gamma and omega
This journey takes us on to the next chakra,

Listen: Intelligence of action at the gates
We form the future of communication
Written to and from our final destination
Looking to the future of a transfiguration
In the hopes of a scripted resurrection
Alchemy between our life's blood and the fates.

This is the lesson of the sacred Kabbala
Taught me from the lips of the blessed Magdala.

Antediluvian Peace

I remember before the enlightenment
When dark caverns held mysterious secrets
There was a cave in a cliff above a river
Sheltered by towering trees
With leaves so lush
They made the darkness of midnight at noon.

And the old folks would stand before the stone
That stood to the left in the doorway to the cave
Reciting verses from days of yore
And the kinsfolk from all around would gather
Singing praises to the stone
Rains would fall so hard
That we would fear for our very lives.

And we would sleep on the ground
Hearing the ancient river roar
Death and time stood still
Creating the space
For grace to abound.

Inner Sanctum

Hey! Everyone who thirsts
Come down to the source and drink your fill
Come down and drink the living water
Without money and without price.

For there is a deeper well-spring
A lake that's calm and bottom-free
The spirit floats, the soul rejoices
In a pure and calm baptismal font.

So rest your heart and slake your thirst
With sacred waters from the fount
Sing the old psalms from days of yore
Immersed amidst eternal balm.

Why buy the common culture's curse
When you can have it all for free?
Wrongs are righted, regrets forgotten

Ides of March on the Left Bank

The waters of the Seine flow swiftly by
Dead souls and bodies perish where they lie
Civilizations grow while people die
And all we give them is a wounded sigh.

They built our world in layers, stone by stone
Brought forth in hardship, bone by bone
We eat their fruit for free, do they condone
By feeding us, do they their lives atone?

Muse not! We make our meanings in this life
And harvest psychic fruit by our own strife,
Together here and now we wield the scythe
And cut each other with the self-same knife.

Our skulls contain an infinite jest
Say those who knows its finite puzzle best
Our death is necessary to our quest
Who bears the burden s(he) is truly blessed.

Job

The heavens declare the glory of God
And the earth is his DIY footstool
But we have the right to question his workmanship
From earthquakes, childhood cancers, to Bonny and Clyde.

I rather think s(he) is omniscient but not omnipotent
What a dilemma s(he) faced in deciding
whether to create anything at all!
Knowing that creation would contain so much evil
And who knows how it might all turn out.

I notice Job got his house and family back
He wound up better off than before
But in the real world it doesn't happen like that.

Oh Lord, hard times have come upon us
Why do you chastise us so?
You'd think that if you really exist
You'd at least let us know
Or give us a short, clear and unambiguous instruction manual.

Since you don't talk to us like you did to the prophets
You'd think we could just forget about you
and go on about our business

But we don't...

Selah

No Man Sees My Face and Lives

Was this the fire in Moses' burning bush
That changed the whole Mediterranean?
Did Moses see behind the veil of truth
The aweful Face that keeps the world aflame?

There's something going on, we know not what
Its mystery is all that we can see,
But deep behind the cloak of normalcy
There's something very strange that's happening here.

What is this blessed water that we drink,
And does it flow from yonder crystal fountain?
And what dread air upon which we breathe
Is it the same as blowed on Calvary?

What's left when all of nature's run its course,
When human bodies and matter decompose?
Except that Holy Ghost that graced His life?
Except that Holy Shroud that draped His Corpse?

The fire is burning still, I see its smoke
Beyond the veil of flesh and drudgery;
I feel the heat and flame and holy fire
O God! Purify me with an awful kiss.

A New Way of Living

I feel a need to be alive anew
To live as if my blood were pure and clean,
And flowing with a love that can be seen
With purpose that my heart can know is true,
With sacredness in all I think and do.
I long to circle my own star, not lean
Towards opinion of what others mean,
To trace the path that I alone can hew.

Not penny, pound, or Euro do I follow
Tradition, custom are for me too narrow.
I follow only my true soul's own arrow
Partaking of my solitude and marrow.

If all else fails me then I have my heart
And nature which I am so much a part.

Point of View

We each are really just a point of view,
  Particular perspective from a point
  Immersed in a totality of wholeness;
Spectacular collective through and through.

  Reality of any one or thing
  Is just as true for me, for one and all.
  I am not limited to what I see and feel
Although my understanding's from afar.

  As long as lover's love in ecstasy,
  As long as life is lived in charity,
No matter where, or when, or who, or what,
  I am complete despite my meager lot.

  But still I recognize that pain exists,
  Injustice too embedded in my bliss.
  The bell that tolls for others tolls for me
  And like a sore it festers all I see.

  But that I think is what a God is for,
  To balance books and even up the score,
To make it all worth more down to the core,
  Though it be on some very distant shore.

And if there be no God forevermore,
Then I say we must do it, you and I,
It matters not how long it takes, bye and bye,
We must become, with mightiest of roar:

A Leveler of last resort,
A host of angels in a final court,
A comforter enough to sift and sort,
To dry up tears, make long what was too short,

A Power bringing universe to port.

Gnosis

I know that there is poetry unheard
Produced at such tremendous bitter cost
That though we never see a single word
We feel its meter, though the sense is lost.

Some say that logic is God's greatest gift
to us; but my computer does that best.
To think is noble but will never lift
An algorithm to its mother's breast.

We're tricked by hormones and our parents' genes
To analyze our thoughts, the inner means
By which we feel; but memes are not the gist;
We only know, and therefore we exist.

Legacy

A million years ago, when earth was young,
Our ancestors created the beginnings;
A home, a hearth, brought forth a mother tongue;
Bequeathed humanity a mind that sings.

Throughout the ages blood, and sweat, and toil
Wrung beauty from the dung-filled soil and clods,
But now we are engaged in new turmoil,
With mindless logic, numbers as our gods,

And information, purposeless, mere chance
Heaps scorn on meaning, turns art to photograph.
But as for me, I choose the human dance,
It's not the destination, it's the path.

If this be error, and so convinced my heart,
I never lived, nor ever worshiped art.

Passion of the Many Worlds

This universe is not our only home
Though it be made by god or quantum foam,
If we exist why not a multiverse
With worlds as blessed as this one's surely cursed?

This broken weary world's a proving ground
For all the dross and beauty to be found,
None but the best and true move up on high
What's gross will wither, fade away and die.

The miracle was beyond our time and space,
A stirring that the void could not erase,
A field of raw potentialities
Bubbling forth infinite realities.

Some worlds like ours have lesser energies,
While others move at higher frequencies
That sin and evil never can abase:
Behold the angels who gaze upon god's face.

New Stuff

Meaninglessness is all there is,
we are engulfed in blackness of night.
Death is in our future, our life is sure to end.
There is no book to set us straight, though many have been written.
The heavens are silent, no voice above is heard.

Somehow a world is here, we are sure that we exist.
The sky is full of stars, galaxies without number.
The earth is full of life, creatures large and small.
Our bodies are a marvel, our minds a mystery.

I feel new stuff in my bones, my blood flows through my brain.
If I'm a simulation, predetermined by a program:
Still I think and feel and am, surely a miracle.
I exult to my programmer, "Hear me shout, hear me, see me, I am."

New stuff.
Carve your ideas into the wood-
Leave your knife stuck in the tree-
Perchance someone in future will find it
and carve marvelous things.
You can always buy a new knife in the city.

The future is the meaning, the meaning is to be created.
I curse the meaningless night. Let this be my epitaph,

"He came forth from the void."

Analects

小　菇

The Priestess

You stood near the fire's shaking air, smoke and ash
Your seersucker skirt fluttering in the breeze
Turned your head to face me, full on, straightaway
Your eyes locked on mine

What quavering thoughts unspoken
Then, today, and tomorrow mourn...

There is No Memory of a Moment

There is no memory of a moment
Only chains of connections in the mind.
Life's no memory, but far more real
Search the brain all you want, it ain't there to find.

For my brain may be puny, and my mind may be small
But my life is a miracle, or not there at all.

The Ant

We are ants living in a hill,
Coordinated motion, never still:
The hive alone has purpose that is real.

I want to be a good little ant
A part of something better, but I can't:
So much trouble, doubt, and fear I feel.

An ant is nothing by itself you see,
The hill is greater than its parts can be:
An ant can't sing, just squeak, so I do squeal.

Blowing in the Breeze

In this fleeting instant, there at my side,
You feel emotions of a thousand years,
And deep within your heart, but inches wide,
You know the joys of angels, and the tears.

Arise, and toss your head from side to side,
And let your hair blow in the breeze;
For only moments can it last, and then
'Twill be but a memory.

Away From All Society

Away from all society,
In a distant woods,
I could gladly be;
By a babbling brook.

Society lasts for but an hour;
Silence lasts for 'aye.
Sweet words soon turn sour;
Babbling brooks remain.

Why should I search the world around
To find my heart's dream,
When flowers abound,
Encircling my feet?

Why should I search both wide and far
For melancholy,
When a fading star
Dies above me now?

If all else fails me, when alone,
Loneliness will do;
A coldness of bone,
A light head, faint heart.

The Goose

A wild goose stopped by
My window to say hello

His big body awkward
But beautiful

We stared at each other for a while
But said not much

For after all, he was a goose
And I a person.

The Path

The way of heaven is a path of love
Not of yourself but of the one above
But if your heart demurs, I do not blame
To tread the path of love is no mere game.

The Restaurant

The rain fell down and made me wet
As I stood outside the restaurant
And stared into the window at comradery.
I longed to share the wine and revelry
But could not spare the change without regret.

A warm fire, a hearth, and friends
Are to be cherished time and time again,
But still the drizzling rain is kind
And wet skin, warm memories, and rain
Bring back other times, and hearths, and fires.

The Wedding

The wedding was a big success
The bride she was alluring
The priest stood tall and talked to all
The groom he was a-glowing.

The church was packed with folks who knew
The future was unknowing
The pictures filled time's static space
The karma was a-flowing.

The friends they came from far and wide
They dropped their daily devotions
To fill a space, a time and place
With unreal, surreal emotions.

Oh! when I look back
In future's past
I'll never know the meaning
We floated in a gleaming fog
Of ever-present seeming.

Glory

Living life in hope of seeing justice done
It has been my sad opinion not true
But words God-spoken men heed not
As prizes such as justice flee hands
Of strong men not weak. But the world

Abides by law, God, and men
In times, there, here abide and keep
Law, token, real in full **Glory**-
And God holds in hand so tight
Men see not, neither understand.

Eyes

Eyes have a piercing way
Cold, efficient, darting;
Or maybe soft and warm,
Human, innocent;
But eyes that pierce
Move men more,
Like rapiers flashing
Quicker than the eye can see.
Eyes are like the coldest lake,
But, oh, too real.

Player Shooting Basketball

Fluid, arched, the bow-bend breaks
Arrow flights to target straight
Retrace path of bending arc
Fall once to earth, bounce cushioned
Repeat in time
Satori of a tranquil mind.

Scar

A scar is time-placed
A junction of the mind
With places meant to be
An ordained sample
Generously clouded into
Our lives and times
To pass, but remain
In our minds, as
Mind and man, flesh
Rot to nothingness.

A distance too large to transgress
A time too mighty to ignore
Our pleasure's fancy whisked away to rest
A hope brought firmly down to nest.

A shout from home of other days
A rendering of soul's first urge
To find and keep it; the call
Imbeds in memory's lost soul.

One World

One world, all people equal calm and free
All cultures and all tongues distinct with dignity

No need to hate the monsters of our history

A world united in diversity
Come quickly! For it is meant to be!

The Mind of God

The mind of God is a perfect place of peace
Where all is reconciled and naught is lost
Where all injustice and sin will surely cease
And this old broken world will be worth the cost.

Jonah

I saw the monstrous beast Leviathan
Spit out the special image of a man
That fought against a creature I was loath
To call the crude and cruelest Behemoth.

The dragon-beast with daring skill was killed,
Its mighty heart forever more was stilled.

We ate the magic fish with fins and scales,
And in Arcadia we told our tales.

Brother of God

We are God's brother, ugly still-born twin,
We know not who to bury, us or Him.
Disfigured, we are left to plan and chart,
While clawing at our casket in the dark.

God of the Gaps

The god of the gaps he gets a bad rap,
Equations work just fine to calculate;
But when it comes right down to my own fate,
Infinity in me is what I map.

Dante Didn't Have an Editor

Dante didn't need an editor.

Brevity

All intelligence is data compression.

The Brain

My brain is a meat machine of mis-matched parts
Cobbled together, a wonder it starts.
Electrical, chemical, reptilian too,
A pinkish-grey pudding of bloody sinew.

The Soul

The soul is a chthonic, tellurian tomb
Deep, dark, and dreary, the womb of our doom;
Entangled roots and creatures, blood and bones,
With runes, hieroglyphics and standing stones.

Time is God

We know that time is God, and God is time
For all can by the clock be fully measured.
Our lives are filled with meter and with rhyme,
Our songs are for their rhythms rightly treasured.

Exorcise

Sometimes life creeps up
Unexpectedly.
No call can exorcise
The life that's nearest Death.

The call is not so wild
As to bring forth remembrance
Of a childhood dream
Forever locked in yesterday.

Spot of Time

The moon gives artificial light
Upon the healthy and the maim
It gives it all through all the night
Forever and for 'aye the same.

The mist hides the outline of the town
Beneath the verdant hill of Adam
Silent clawing of a multitude
To gain access to a spot of time.

The Sparrows

You are worth many sparrows
One in a million is not zero
There are no hopes to spare, Oh!
Consider Pascal, not Nero.

The Crow

Your basic crow, it is no dummy bird.
I dare to venture that at least a third
Know right from wrong; and will always survive
'Spite slings and arrows, singing subtle songs.

Reality

Life is but a waking dream,
A hope embodied, a visible thought.
Therefore, do not search to find the morrow,
But write your songs with fingers in the sand,
And like Sir Spens, go walking on the strand.

Time

Time is the stuff nightmares are made of.
Every passing second is an eternity
Of shame, horror, and pain.
Time creeps on ever slower
Like a ball rolling uphill.
Time is what we wish we had more of
Though every moment is a baptism of fire.

I've Lived in Time

I've lived in time for all my natural life,
Pierced by her prong-like ever-present claws,
That slice my heart, my bowels, my inner entrails,
Like razor-sharpened, always-active saws.

Imprisoned in her lair with no escape,
Held fast between her cat-quick subtle paws,
With nowhere else to turn, I raise my eyes,
To gaze into her masticating jaws.

It Has to Make Sense

God is a law maker, not a law breaker
Miracles happen because the law rhymes
And not because of broken laws or crimes.

Symbols

Engage with symbols at your own peril!
They care not whose body and blood are sacrificed.
The holy bread and wine are often crushed
Into the perfect figure of a Christ.

We wear a crown of thorns upon our brow
Yoked to our crosses like oxen to a plow.

Paradise

Passionate flowers, with butterflies in flight
And puppies bouncing all around a stream
That gurgles o'er smoothly well-worn rocks
The morning songbirds chortling with delight.

Zeitgeist

So why can't we make great art anymore
  Like ancient seers and poets of yore?
Our verses and songs are feeble and frail
  Pale homages to hoary prophets' lore.

We are seeking the Master's holy grail
  In the environs of old Israel.

Done in by Algorithms

I am the last human poet
Shed a tear for me anon.
Better verses via algorithms
By computers will be done.

I am an epiphenomenon,
A ghost in a machine.
I laugh, I cry, I bleed, I die,
Directed by my genes.

My mind soars in the heavens
I dream in movie reels,
Roboticised, lobotimized,
But that's not how it feels.

Maybe I am controlled by my genes'
Chemical factors and physical schemes,
Nonetheless in one of my myriad dreams
I had an original and partial thought-shell,
Figment of a fragment of a novel idea
That unrighteously presumes to be
Someday just a bit more
Than it seems.

The Map is not the Territory

People may say
"Certainly! Certainly!"
But there is no certainty
The Truth is also a Lie

I want to say something
But what do I talk about?

Language is not Reality.

Amen

So!
The world is passing strange
The world eats us
We cut, we break, we separate and differentiate
We join together
We moan, we anguish, we articulate
The world eats us
We eat the world
Let it be
So be it.

Gilgamesh

We are all Zombies
But if we hold hands
And share our bread and share our blood
We may be resurrected.

The Sun Also Rises

Baha'u'llah, the clouds are clearing
I can see the sun arising
And the mountain peaks appearing
As a brand new day is dawning.

A babe is born to blessed Magdala
As foretold by sacred kabbala
Looking to a future transfiguration
Earth's soul reborn, reconsecration.

From the deep heart of spiritus mundi
Comes the return of long sought Mahdi
From Mt. Moriah's sacred chakra
Fulfillment of our ancient karma.

The wanderer has finally found a home
In Carmel's majestic golden dome.

Elsie Vanover, nee Crabtree

Little money. Little status.
Hard Work. Hard Life.
Dirt farmer. Nature Lover.
People talker, person mother.
Death at hand.

"The color. The colors.
The flowers. The flowers.
The music...
The song!..."

Meandering

a stream has its own direction, none can gainsay it
its choice is its flow, is its pattern, its way, its meaning, its course
a river is right
it has nothing to confess or be forgiven
it is perfect, blameless, omnipotent
a river is satisfied, justified, indemnified.

The Ocean

blue green blue iridescent sparkling waves
lapping the shore, licking the rocks, loving the sand
God-given sacred blood of earth
teaming with life-forms of a million years' worth
soaking up the sun and suckling the moon
more complex than a human life. More meaning than a billion stars

Time vs. Space

Time has never been defeated, tamed, or fenced in.
Time is more fundamental than space.
If you had space but no time, nothing could exist;
If you had time but no space, consciousness could exist.

Pura Vida

Mon Dieu, I bow, force majeure
Alive, to be, to strive
The cross, the blood, a Dios
L'chaim, to rhyme, sublime.

Chaos and the Law of Love

Chaos drives the crossroads of life,
The Law of Love's your only map and guide.
Each turn of the road, each fork of the way,
If it doesn't help others, it's not OK.
God's infinite justice and infinite mercy,
Wherever God wants you is where you'll be.

Chaos drives the crossroads of life.

On Getting Old

Well, I'm just like an old lump of coal,
With fire down deep in my soul.
My heart's a fiery ember,
I barely can remember
When my forest was as green as gold.

Kenosis

Embrace the mystery
Throw yourself into the uncertainty
Eat the paradox
And digest the unthinkable.

L'Chaim.

The Friend

To a friend
Who was strong
Though perhaps not wise
To a friend, I say
Though perhaps at times
Enemies
We were.

No Apologies

Mother, I long for your smile,
Savannah, I long for your touch,
Calliope, I long for your memory.
The sound of silence in my brain is terrifying.

No apologies.
Pero, lo siento.
Mais, je suis desolee.
Mea culpa.

Amen.

The Heavens Declare the Glory of God

Vaulting across the rosy-fingered dawn
Splashing stars across the night's dark dome
Dark thunderclap and cloud's prodigious doom
Dazsizzling of the sun as noon time zooms

Oak

Open field
Big tree
Flowing upwards
Shading the sun
Sturdy
Solid bark against the world.

Death's Head

So soon to die a natural death
A death's head on the table,
I wish I'd been a troubadour
Or Viking hailing shores.

The sun is setting, and my thoughts
Are going down again.
Until their essence dwindles
Like a flame expiring slowly
In a sudden, defiant death.

Manifesto

小 菇

The Jazz Combo

I listened to a jazz combo the other night
Led by a piano player who was out of sight,
He controlled the band with his eyes and he had a mustache
He was cool, calm, collected, and playin' for cash.

The piano player was sober and so was the bass
Who was tall and slender with emotionless face.
The drummer was older, drinking 151
You could tell he didn't believe in anything new under the sun.

They'll tell you it's sex, drugs, & rock and roll
As if all you had to do was play from your soul,
They say it's the imperfections that make the song
But try it very long and you'll find they're wrong.

They weren't no quintet with two saxophones
Just a trio of losers and total unknowns.

Breed

What breed are you? What breed am I? That breed
That binds you and defines you is a brand
For all to see, burned into your hide,
A badge of honor or dishonor, not earned
But deeper than the skin and wider than the sky.
The only thing I want from breed is to be freed.

You are tex and I am mex and your sex
Is there to behold you to a role
You never sought to own. Your very soul
Is not your own when passersby can own
Your smile and peg you to a country mile.
I am more than where I'm born and what I wear.

Some are born both high and low, and why?
If our great land is for all and free
For people to rise and fall then why oh why
Is one rich daughter a thoroughbred
While others are stuck sucking hind tit?
Either we are humans all or else iconoclasts.

The world is wide the world is round, we all
Float on the edge, equidistant from the core,
We will be wed to fairness, not bred to market
We must be fed with milk of human kindness
Not hired and sired like studs and breeding mares.
Our destiny is to define our own histories.

We

Oh God, why do you vex us so?

We who have toiled in the vineyards of the Lord
We who have eaten our bread by the sweat of our brow
We who have stamped out the vintage of the grapes of wrath.

We who are not academics and who did not graduate
From the Iowa Writer's Workshop
We who are not intellectuals nor shapers of opinion
We also need to sing our songs and write our poems.

We serve the coffee and clean the tables
We are not the rockstars nor the athletes
We are lost in a faceless sea of billions of people
We whose prayers are never answered.

Did we not worship you in fear and trembling?
Did we not call upon your name in praise?
Did we not search for you diligently?
Did we not seek you in all reverence?

We feel the pain and humiliation
We feel the shame and senselessness
We feel the agony of defeat
We feel abused and neglected.

Will we not be here still tomorrow?
Will we not bleed in silence then also?
Will we not weep forever more?

Oh God, why do you chastise us so?

Dark Night of the Soul

In midst of silent night my mind does soar
To topics, always hid in joyful day,
That only night time's silence, and the sway
Of memories I thought I knew no more,
Could bring me to take up the bitter chore.
I think of chances I have thrown away
And love that should be gone, but begs to stay.
Then all the night I stand upon the shore
Of life's sad sea, and watch the silent waves.
I wonder why all things so swiftly pass
As do the dying waves, to nothingness;
I ask myself why all that my soul craves
Is in the unreachable past. Alas!
For gone is all my former happiness.

Armageddon

When quakes shall root out foundings to the core,
When bold Abora shakes with cholic roar,
Then let the one in Caledonia weep
That man so rashly lays him down to sleep.

How small a loss it were to lose a race
Of mighty mind and self-assured face,
Who write their songs with fingers in the sand,
And like Sir Spens, go walking on the strand

Yet still a pity should we lose our hope,
Our grandiose, death-defying hope,
The wondrous fever of the human show,
Incessant questing, time always our foe...

Before the solemn eyes of aged Pope
Man holds the last spectacular at bay.
No more we weep; the moon is full again
Today; Eternity is then tomorrow.

Meta-Art

The rosy-fingered dawn's a metaphor
For human culture in my psychic pores,
And all that poetry's a stand-in for
From Homer's sacred wine dark shores.

For all the world's a stage, a tragedy,
A mental liquor, deep inside of me
With full Shakespearean majesty,
As long as I have art and poetry.

And thus when life, so petty and uncouth
Haunts me; it's Keats's purple-stained mouth
That soothes me with its mystic truth,
Consolation from the mythic South.

Life sucks. The only tonic I can find:
The magic and the meaning in my mind.

New Orleans

I've never been to New Orleans
I still don't know just what that means
She has never left the town
She wears its mask and frighted frown.

Our fathers had blood on their hands
As they came from distant lands
Our mothers had the moon in their hair
As they entered Eden fair.

Our past was blank and paperwhite
As we set forth that fateful night
We were their children, slave, and king
What would the unknown future bring?

Down on the levee there I heard a cry
Deep in the city where the crowd stood nigh
Out in heart of darkness land
Near where Custer made his stand.

Out where Denver's mountains start
On high desert plains we fell apart
It's there we'll make a brand new start
At Wounded Knee you'll find my heart.

It was in the afternoon of our delight
There was no one left we had to fight
Except the ghosts of ancient ancestors
Piled high in whited sepulchers.

Cities of the Damned piled high
Life is wet but Death is dry
Until the flood comes racing in
And mixes silt and bones and sin.

On Bourbon Street we faced our fear
Down by the darkened river near
Where on Canal Street we felt her breath;
Life smells strongest nearest Death.

The one-eyed Gypsy blew her futile horn
The undertaker listened, showing her his scorn
Somewhere in the distance, a little babe was born
Listen to the whistle blow, futile and forlorn.

I've never been to New Orleans
I still don't know just what that means
I'll always see her from afar,
With all her rainbows and her scars...

The Path of Love

To tread the path of love one must believe,
It takes a leap of faith to be born again,
You must believe in something to be saved,
Even if belief is in belief itself.

What counts is not the dogma but the way,
So, why all the different dogmas?
Because we are not animals you see,
Because with no beliefs we are just monsters.

You must believe in life to be alive,
You must believe in meaning to have hope,
You must believe in purpose to have a soul,
You must believe in love to be a human.

So, if you really need a dogma,
Please choose a kinder, gentler one,
And just believe and keep on going
Believe and work your miracles slow and sure.

The Miracle

A miracle does not depend
On the vicissitudes of people.
A miracle is the difference
Between a mathematical description
And the suchness of a thing.

The difference between an approximation
And an exactitude.
A leap across a chasm
From doubt to certitude.

From the ugliness of contingency
To the sweetness of the spirit.
From utter nothingness
To complete loveliness.

A miracle is the existence of anything
Much less a universe, planets and people.
A miracle is your life
And your interactions with other people.

A miracle is a man with no power
Who lived a short life
And died a criminal's death,
Who changed the world.

A miracle is when you realize
That existence is sacred,
That every hair is numbered
Like every grain of sand.

There is a World

There is a world of emerald and green
Where empathic people go home to be free.

There is a world, it's one of a kind
Where posters of art forms explode in the mind.

I jump and I fly up above the moon
Reading the signs like alien runes.

You and I are reeling in the reverie of youth
The circus of beholding underground truth.

There is a world where children can play
And bring back from the beach a seal for the day.

There is a world where spirits can roam
And unwanted children can go to be home.

There is a world, I know it is true
Where all you got to do is be you.

Remembering the Future

So any being sufficiently advanced
Is indistinguishable from a God,
This universe was created by a God
So God's an artist, the universe his art.

Beginning with a violent big bang
An expanding light cone gyre shoots forth
A spiraling of possibilities
As quantum time unfolds by decoherence.

So time is real but encapsulated
In hyperreal outside of time and space
A vector vertex, a chaotic vortex
With infinite room for free-will histories.

Boundary conditions at the end of time
Attract, reverse the gyre and close the egg
Ensuring equitably good outcomes
And compensate the existence of evil.

A translucent egg with incandescent skeins
A virtual vase with violet flowers
With arteries, veins and scars, traces and trails
Of trillions of lives, species known and unknown.

A mediocre artist would be tempted
To constantly interfere with his
Unfolding art-egg, imposing miracles,
But God builds in vitality to evolve.

He does all this to allow creation
Of excellence and beauty beyond measure
Sparrows and nightingales singing in the trees
Beautiful melodies blowing in the breeze.

God empowers creation with life itself
A virtual reality art-egg gyre
A bulging, pulsing, light-filled obloid
A multimedia Faberge egg.

All good is preserved, all evil is resolved
History meets destiny, at God's Omega Point.
Beauty is truth, and truth is good, that's all
We need to know about God's Greatest Art Work.

Benediction

Yes! I'm at life's ecstatic reunion
Yes! I'm at love's ecstatic reunion
I'm part of all that lives on God's green earth
I'm part of what it means and what it's worth.

There's something going on, it's happening
From slumber we are now awakening
A spirit world is busy now a-borning.
We'll recognize its shape some happy morning.

But when I'm dying I will see its colors
And on my deathbed I will see its flowers.

Disappointment

Maybe the Buddha understood it best,
Desire's the root of all our disappointments,
So relax, calm down, and accept your fate,
Relinquish all desires and meditate.

But then I rather think we westerners
Would find no satisfaction in that route.
We stretch for goals and strive to wrestle angels,
We weigh results and tally up the scores.

We seem to feel that life should offer more,
And worse, we sore regret what we have missed.
We blame our natures, goad our future selves,
Make sick our spirits for our consciences' sake.

Sometimes I relish in my disappointment,
Squeezing its roots to find the inner sauce,
I grimace as I suck its bitter flavor
While savoring the vile and sour bile.

On my deathbed, I'll neither know nor care
If no one reads my scribbled shards of verse.
Are poets, when dead, happy they're in print?
Or are regrets, too, carried in the hearse?

Somehow that thought does not fill me with dread,
My soul's repose is certain when I'm dead,
Last words can't be rescinded nor resaid,
I'll find my satisfaction now instead.

Chronicles

They said we were dead, but we're not dead.
We sleep in your towns, we walk in your streets,
The past is alive, our ghosts see your sins,
You think you're so smart, but you're due for a fall.

We'll bury you along with us,
Our actions, thoughts and consciences
Will haunt and smother your spirits,
We'll blanket you with suffocation
In your lamentation cities.

Your problems are big, they won't go away
Until you realize, your values are wrong.
You kill and you steal, you curse and you swear,
You have no beliefs, you have no ideals.
Money's your god, and play is your prayer,
Your greed and your pride, your sex and your lust
Will bring down the wrath of God and of us
Until you see the Way, and follow the Tao
With contrite hearts and humble minds
And listen to your inner voices
Cherish and honor your heritage
And the Will of Heaven.

You kill your children, adulterate your wives,
You worship money, idolize power,
Your might makes right, and so you laugh.
Your pride goeth before your fall,
You sin before your days of woe.

Your science is perverted,
Your schools are compromised.
Everybody does his own thing,
Each self her own commandments.

How long before your end is come
Before the wrath of God is shown?
Surely your end shall be as Sodom
And your ruins as Gomorrah.
You shall mourn your self-made doom
And wear sack cloth and ashes.

Your problems are big and complex
But the solution's small and simple.
Return to your values, your roots,
Embrace your ethical heritage,
That your days may be as before
And your tomorrows better still.
Repent your lascivious ways,
Respect and obey the Ancient of Days,
Behold the Man of Galilee
And then you will blessed be.

Lamentations

We live in a Zombie civilization
We're soldiers of a Zombie nation
Ruled by money, class, and power
Before the which we crouch and cower.

Would you rather be rich, run a conglomerate,
Over money, men completely dominant?
From the need to succeed there is no hiatus
Controlled by the exigencies of success.
Pyramid's peak is easily replaced
But not so easy the lowly base.

Look around and perceive a very bad world
Cry and grieve for a very sad world
Strive to become a true somebody
Only to become a new nobody.

I am a robot, no doubt in the least
Programmed by chance until I'm deceased.

Stone Cold Sober

The world we see is but a shiny surface
Perhaps to shield us from a fiery furnace.

Yet rip the veil, you'll see a fire burning
Consuming you and all the world before it
The quaking air is like a gyre turning
Tornado winds so strong none stand before it
Dark smoke and ashes pose a dire warning
The demons dance a dirge as they adore it
In time to wailing angel's lyres yearning.
A tune so awful nothing can atone it.

Peer deep into the funeral pyre's churning
Perchance to pierce symbolic higher learning.

Water

It flows between my fingers
Satisfies my skin
It fills any hole
And bends without breaking

You can drink it or mix it
Watch it move or freeze it solid
Boil it away
Or swim in it all day

The space between everything
Is a flowing stream
The secret shape of God
The one eternal flow.

Trinity

Three in one
One in three
When one is short
The two are long
When one is long
The two are short
Filled emptiness
Relationship itself
They turn a circle
And hold up the world.

Birdsong

Birdsong is my favorite thing
I love them singing wing to wing,
A canopy from tree to tree
A musical cacophony.

The sun has dawned the day at last
Some worms and bugs will break their fast,
Their little lives won't last too long
And so they start their day with song.

A bird is simple, small and sweet
I love their tiny little feet,
They have their own community
Overheard by fools like me.

If humans never ever were
No consciousness, no poems to serve
As records of the birds above,
Their world would still be filled with love.

To put it all in simple words,
God did it right, he made the birds.

Float Like a Butterfly

Float like a butterfly, sting like a bee
When you're in love with a life by the sea
Use all your assets, set your soul free
God says that's how your life's supposed to be.

Troubles will find you wherever you go
Don't let the devils disrupt your life's flow
Dance like a tiger, put on a show
Punch like a fighter, go toe to toe.

God says that's how your life's supposed to be
Float like a butterfly, sting like a bee.

Sheer Chaos

Sheer chaos rules the world yet for a season,
The spirit guides the waves, but does not control.
Though we be mired in shallow muddy shoals
Without a rudder and no clarifying reason
Still subtle currents steer us to our goals.

Chaotic waters birth a plenitude.
So as we curse and struggle with the tides
And by mere stars traverse the ocean wide,
Always recall with healthy gratitude
That in the spirit's hope we do abide.

There's something going on here, a commutation.
As we evolve, what will we turn to be?
Transmuted by an inner alchemy,
Effulgence of the soul's transfiguration.

Real Time Blues

A day, a week, a month, a year, I never knew how fast time flew,
I turned around and it was gone, before I could explore,
I couldn't grasp the world at all, while it was fresh and new,
If I could do it all again, I'd pay attention more.

The first time that I heard the blues, I shook from head to toe,
I felt emotions in my heart, I'd never felt before.
I should have lingered longer there, but yielded to life's flow,
Oh! I'd like to do it all again, but pay attention more.

I lived right through the Sixties, on streets and avenues,
Change held me in its power, culture in its groove,
I knew that time was special, but not how fast it flew,
Well if I could live it over, I'd pay attention more.

First time I got religion, I was certain I was right,
My mind was satisfied, I was sure I knew the score,
My soul at peace with living, no one I had to fight,
But if I could do it over, I'd pay attention more.

Now when I'm on my deathbed, what will I think of then?
Will my foundation stand, when I'm at heaven's door?
Will I regret what I have been, and every kind of sin?
Or would I do it all again, and pay attention more?

Sometimes I want to sing the blues,
but the words they just won't come,
I hear them clearly in my sleep, as from a distant shore,
The melody so plain and pure, that I begin to hum,
Oh! I'd like to hear it one more time, but pay attention more.

Mama, ever since you passed away, I often think of you,
And all the things I'd like to say, if we could meet once more,
If I could see you by and by, I know just what I'd do,
I'd give it one more try, and pay attention (just a little bit) more.

Fable

When Homer wrote his lyrics in his mind
Did men take note?
Or did the sky resound, did birds proclaim
The words that Virgil wrote
When life was calm and young?

For birds do sing always,
And subtle undertones resound
In the evening air.
A symphony in harmony
Except for little nuances of sound
That make the whole more perfectly profound.

I wait for nothing but the darkness to confound
I sleep in fear of dying in a swound
In senseless languor of a type of hope
Rejecting what is best for love of life.

Ten times ten I've senseless dead incensed
The raving darkness of a night at peace.
To see the hope of ages all undone
A swirl of light from crystal sparkling sun.

Sol

Home again, a scepter of light
Lovely apparition of delight
I see and understand
As hope takes flight.

All the love in your heart
Is like a crystal beat
Of sound that is not music
But unmelodious tapping
Of some rhythm of the soul.

Let not the sounding madness
Send a dart into your soul
Let not the startling silken magic
Sprinkle dust into the bowl
Of a thousand falling high notes
In a rising watched-for Sol.

Lights in Line Down Lane

Lights in line down lane
Stretching to infinity
With endless stories manifold
Caressing single homes.

Looking over lines of light
In night-time revery
Jealous of the over-ripe
Splendor of storied sleep.

Lights in line down lane
Patterned in a hopeless maze
Singly scattered helter-skelter
In exact displaced design.

Schadenfreude

Was God alive when children bled and died
And anguished mothers bowed their heads and cried?
God lived in Newtown, died in Sandy Hook.
Does God know how much he screwed us up
When he made the world and messed it up
And for guidance left a holy book?

I was the geek who others cursed and scorned
Was not with beauty or with friends adorned.
I am other, you love to spit on me.
I was the nerd, the weakling vampire boy
Whose lowly status fed communal joy
So you could lord and lady be...

We are ants living in a hill,
Coordinated motion, never still:
The hive alone has purpose that is real.
I want to be a good little ant
A part of something better, but I can't:
So much hatred, pride, and greed I feel.
An ant is nothing by itself you see,
The hill is greater than its parts can be:
An ant can't sing, just squeak, so I do squeal.

Ode to the Baby Boomer Generation

Mourning for an elegy of fortune unreceived,
Mourning for a legacy of destiny deceived;
Like Mozart, too early felled by fickle hand of fate,
Mourning for what they could not comprehend nor consummate.

Stitched in between the times, a momentary suture,
Out of touch with the past, yet still not a part of the future.

Like vampires, not still alive, but merely yet undead,
Their mountains still unclimbed, their stories left unsaid;
Forever on the cusp of expectations unachieved;
Forever on the cusp of what they never could achieve.

A Night of Silence

A night of silence dulls the brain
Like murder of our consciousness.
The stain of death is on our minds
Dissolving through osmosis of the soul.

No sharp-black refining of the mind
To rapiers like the lightening
Here and gone, no time to think
Intelligence of action at the gate.

No, a dull-brown sleepiness
Creeping about as if an itching
Spread slowly across the skin:
To die without the wonder of it.

Postmodern Transportation

Tin can, bomb on back, barbaric way to fly,
Strapped in, barely breathing, shooting through the sky.
No control, no escape, eight miles high,
Like animals, de-humanized, on our way to die.

Economy class citizens, used to the misery
Screeching through a painful insect ecstasy.

Red Black of Night

I went down to the ship
where my family was stripped
and I knew that the air was all wrong.
Sumer and Tyre
they hung like a wire
and at night the red star was full strong.
Gone halfway from home
from Egypt and Rome
and the ground was infirm where I stepped.
Looked back to the East
Where lay the dead beast
and I knew why my mother had wept.

The baby was nigh
but no shepherds on high
and no Place I could call all my own.
Deep down in the ice
we all tossed the dice
to see what our futures had shown.
My nerves they were shot
By her breath so damn hot
and down by the river it flowed
Wet, black and ripe
it felt so damned right
but by blood was the baby dethroned.

The battle is waged
With sulfur and rage
in the place where the future is found.
The eagle does soar
The green grass grows o'er
The blood of my dad in the ground.
I've been here so long
In river and song
That I don't recognize my own ghost.
My feet in the sand
I'm stuck on this strand
Of forsaken, forgotten coast.

Red like the Nile
Dry with denial
like Jason I sailed in the night.
Spread sheepskin to fate
Two days I did wait
With stars it is useless to fight.
Was here I was born
and here I still mourn
Three days was the babe out of sight.
The brew I did sip
Cursed be the ship
Engulfed me in red black of night.

Consilience ex Nihilo

Nihilism, Nihilism
Is what it comes down to,
An infinite variety
Of language, song, and art,
And all we have to show for it
Is dancing in the dark.
A universe of broken dreams
It could be more or less,
A little space of consciousness,
And the rest is silence-
Our brains refuse to believe it though,
We cannot let it go;
A brain's a prism, turning nothing
Into a real rainbow.

Night-Wanderer

The nights of many towns I've known
Some are slow, some are short
And some from tempest fires have grown
Some are docile, love's cohort.

I love to walk, to measure towns
Through silent empty streets
The houses full of gay nightgowns
Whisper to all they meet.

One sees the scenes of day be still
Beneath beholding stars
And ponders on the moon until
A realization jars

Him into kinship with the night.
He sees his fitful state
His life, a lonely one-chance fight
Beneath the stars of fate.

Blue

Soft phantom yellow, smoothly curved
A wing, frail, silent, still
A butterfly in motion, time forgot
Tomorrow is our yesterday
Flying, sing in whispers
Murmur of tomorrow in the sky
Silken wings beat softly
Tufts of air are churned in time
Until tomorrow steals the scepter
As a bluish motion squeezes in
To cover yellow paper in a daze
Of dreaming memory, blue is real.

To the Maiden

Of all the maidens fair who have been crowned
By sweetest Venus, with a wreathe of beauty,
It's you alone, with tender melancholy,
Knows bittersweet compassion, so profound,
You cast your eyes down to the sullen ground,
Recalling the sweet-sad memory
Of hopeless love's torturous melody.
Ah! What sad romance is in mem'ry found
That does not change the heart for good or ill,
That it be not the same forever more?
When judgment comes, and secrets all are shown,
Will not a grievous wound be found there still?
Could not our Maker in our heartstrings' lore
Read all our sorrows, 'til our lives be known?

A Moment's Quietly Turned Masterpiece

A moment's quietly turned masterpiece
Stray straws together in the wind
More beautiful because it has to cease
More perfect since it's destined soon to end.

Minute design, in shapeless details wrought
Yet by some artist's accidental deed
A lovely whole, a curve, just as if sought
A bosom beauty, sprung from heaven's seed.

A thing so lovely of itself must be
A token from that other spectral land
Where love is real and by a roaring sea
Nymphs write their songs with fingers in the sand.

So soon to fade, yesterday is never,
Love me now, for this is our forever.

Obsession

A strange lady of the night
Tripping back and forth at ease
With nature's gloomy scene
No troubles on the placid screen or mask.

"Consciousness is the continent of love"
She says, idly watching rising moon
"Life is but a dream of love"
Lifting of her skirt that trails.

Lovely woman of l'amour?
Or questionable virtue or grace?
The eyes enticing, strange, so dark
The night is but her shadow on the moon.

Lovely woman of l'amour
Why laugh and play so gay
Know not there lives within ourselves
A dark and sordid beast?

Not so, for throughout
The wild and jagged slopes
Live certain strains of din
That shake within and smooth
Without. So let it be
That lovely uses shape their own
And you, lonely traveler
Shall sing in doubt
Of Kilimanjaro.

A moment wasted never more returns
And tasks done well are rare
And burdensome.
But on this night I care
But little for the best
And small I make of wind
That's raging, vagabond
About our nestling perch.

Judge not harshly, nor in anger,
For I am but a man in search
Of what I am,
And where I go.
How I love you'll never know.

You know not why I turn away,
It's not as seems,
I'm well aware
You're but inches from my side.

Shall I, deferentially, try
To please in everything I do,
Unnatural,
Although harmless
As a painting on the wall?

I must be me, and yet it hurts
To be seen in this sordid light.

Let me but ask
"Do you love me?"
Eternity is then tomorrow.

Damsel, weep not.
I know you're there.
If I but knew your thoughts,
In this instant,
Of the quaking earth around the flaming fire.

Without a name I met you in the green,
I lost my sense, I told you I was me.
No matter now.
I kneeled and whispered to the night,
Against the stars its useless that one fight.

I love Madame; I saw her once
With hair down in the breeze,
And all her stars and bells, they waved
And tinkled merrily.

I saw her once again, quite soon
And found her in a daze.
She saw the air, its shaking quake
And told the story well.

I saw her once again, once more,
And knew it was a dream,
For things that leave us softly ill
Are not reality.

Woman, your beauty is a soul.
Your troubled eyes ponder
All around.

I cannot reprove you
If you cast your love away
For life is not a game

You once were simple
But now, because your beauty shows,
The world is at your feet.
You're troubled, there's no doubt,
Though taking pleasure is easy.
You are not corrupted,
But you cannot withstand the will
And the way of the world.
What will you turn to be?

"I haven't even done it" she said
As if the world were waiting.
All rolled up, the over-question
"Is it done?" Oh, no.
The question isn't even asked
And time shall roll it under dust
Until even I won't recognize
"I haven't even done it"
And time rolls on downhill
Further in escape and imprison
Me in my yesterdays.

Damsel, serene nights
Are not conducive to you
In my thoughts. Tonight,
Serene reflections cast doubt
Upon your perfect visage
Marring unserene wake
Of emotions with placid
Thought-shells.

Perhaps the future will bring
A hope, renewal
Of a love unrequited

But real, strong
And uncontrolled.

Shall one so lovely in a day
Reject the winds of healing grace?
Can patterned motion, love's caress
Seal up inside a cocoon's nest?

Can beauty die, in coldness still
A corpse in silence of repose?
Can breathing cease, the chest be numb
A swollen hole of emptiness?

Unreachable star!
The all in all.
Naught else can suffice.
In this instant,
Still can I see your shadow
And touch the hem of your skirt
Failure is exalted
To the all in all.

Together we could glide into oblivion
And drown our sorrows in the wine of failure.

Israel

We made it to the homeland of the grail,
The holy land of Eretz Yisrael,
But I was not a perfect spotless calf,
And so like Sarah I just had to laugh.

Israel, Israel, where did I go wrong?
And where are the answers I have sought so long?
My soul is wounded, my spirit gone astray,
There is no balm in Gilead today.

Backwater City, Nazareth, Galilee,
A million miles from nowhere, just like you and me,
But all the patriarchs and angels still confess
The rock of Judah in the wilderness.

I've been to Elijah's cave in Mount Carmel,
There's been no time to think since Cain killed Abel,
When time's immortal curtain passes by
The future's smokey shadows freeze and die.

From Nebo on Pisgah I spied the Jordan,
The valleys of Jezreel and Armageddon,
The spirits of the dead floated in the air
Where ancient armies clashed with hope and despair.

Young Jacob walked aloof in Palestine,
He wrestled in his dreams with the divine,
Created a notion of a different kind,
And Israel became a conscious mind.

But what weird creatures we have now become!
I feel my death before my time has come,
We see that minds are gods, and God is one,
So am I cursed, or am I a chosen one?

I am a void that walks and talks and cares,
I have emotions that I cannot share,
You look at me and you see nothing but I swear
I look inside and I see being there.

The gods are all dead, with none to be found,
Bethel is empty, in Shiloh no sound,
From Hebron to Zion and on to the sea,
Swing low to the Jordan and set my soul free.

Say, "mene, mene, tekel, decided,
Your days are numbered, counted, weighed and divided."
God's finger has guided and amply provided,
His grace has sufficed and unto us abideth.

When David saw Bathsheba bathe alone,
Her husband killed, then shared his bed and throne,
A son was sired, because he was enticed,
And from this union descended Jesus Christ.

All I can say, is Oh Lord, I hear,
So hear, O Israel, I will always fear,
With trembling I will wait for you to appear,
While trusting deep inside that you are near.

Jerusalem, Jerusalem, not yet
To reach and walk your streets I sore regret,
But I'm exhausted by the vision and I weep,
For all the promises I couldn't keep.

Jerusalem, city of blood and death,
We each will reach you with our dying breath,
And see the light of Zion face to face,
And shed our life's blood in this aweful place.

Moriah, I am sacrificed to you,
My soul is bound and bared on top of you,
Where multitudes of people have been killed,
On your blood-devouring sacred hill.

We're chosen all of us but we must too
Cross over the Jordan as true Hebrews,
And enter a strange land we never knew,
We're chosen but we're under judgement too.

Suffering, suffering, endlessly be,
Nailed to the cross of an agony tree,
Our souls are blood-pressed on Gethsemane,
'Til death brings relief and sets the soul free.

The evil is necessary, but one must sustain,
And run a good race in spite of the pain.
But all shall be well, yes, all shall be well,
And all manner of things shall be well.

City of light and gold and diamonds sublime,
Beyond all reason and rhyme at the end of time,
Peace will be found in New Jerusalem,
You're assured your shalom in Yerushalayim.

You're assured your shalom in Yerushalayim.

Scribblings on the Ceiling

It's like we're fighting for the attention of God
All people, plants and things are fighting
To gain the attention of an eye in the sky
That notices beauty, form and meaning.
Why else do we strive, do birds sing
Atoms dance and stars shine
Galaxies form and crystals constellate?

We all are fighting for the attention of God
We build our castles in our own mind's eye
Shown only to the Holy Spirit's gaze
To gain approval from the One above.

If only one thing keeps us going
The LORD God above will rightly judge.

Apple Dog Blues

I'm walkin' down the road with an apple to eat
A dog at my side and the world at my feet.
Life is short and there's no time to lose
I might as well like it do the apple dog blues.

Goin' down to the creek where the water is wet
There ain't nothin' there that I haven't seen yet.
Life's a bit like a big pig in a poke
It's really hard to handle and it might be a joke.

When I was young, I thought I knew the score
I was eager to brag but now I know more.
As I got older, I opened my eyes
There ain't nothin' dumber than a man who is wise.

Mom was right and Pop was too
My oh my how the years have flew.
But I had great times with Mary Lou
When my blood was fresh and cherry new.

Life is wet but death is dry
Cities of the dead are pilin' high
Sin is wet, but honor dry
The dam's gonna break and the truth is nigh.

I got an apple and a dog and the blues in my head
In my shoes and in my bed.
Life ain't easy and there's no time to lose
I might as well like it do the apple dog blues.

So soon to die a natural death
I feel it with each precious breath.
So soon to die a natural death
I felt it from my very first breath.

Packin' my boots, they're all I'll need
Dreamin' my dreams and my thoughts are freed.
Leavin' in the mornin', I won't be late
Got a real hot date with Father Fate.

Got a meetin' on the mountain with Sister Moon
Got a feelin' that I'll find her really soon.
Got a feelin' this is what our lives are for
Got a feelin' that my cup is brimmin' o'er.

I got a cap on my head and some rags on my back
There ain't nothin' good that I really lack.
The Lord is my God and His waters are pure
The Lord is my God and His mercies are sure.

Apple dog blues are in my head
In my shoes and in my bed.
Life is short and there's no time to lose
You might as well like it do the apple dog blues.

Oh, the apple dog blues are in my head
In my shoes and in my bed.
Life is short and there's no time to lose
You might as well like it do the apple dog blues.

Conceptual Thought

Conceptual thought is my guidance, so I will thrive.
Concepts make me to be always content
And help me to enjoy the rest of sleep.
My very inner being is refreshed,
I walk in knowledge that my path is true.
Though tempests dire surround on every side,
I am serene; my soul is centered,
My mind is calm, my spirit is sufficed.
I am rewarded far beyond my just deserts,
Truth and good abound forevermore
And I exalt eternally in thought.

It's Not What You Think

Let us not be troubled nor dissemble
Over belief and dogma, 'twixt me and you;
The devils also believe and tremble,
It isn't what you think, it's what you do.

The Mouse

As I lay down my pen, should I
Have never picked it up?
Should only those with skill write verse
While others dare not speak?

My tongue and mind are slow but still
My soul has treasures too,
It bids my tongue to prophesy
Though it be with but a squeak.

I write my verse in valid blood
Because it is my own.
I sing my songs with my own voice
My own authentic squeal.

Meditations
小　菇

Reason, Science, Religion, God

What's Going on Here?

What's going on here?

We find ourselves as conscious creatures who are curious about what's going on. We ask questions. How did we get here, what does it all mean? We have succeeded in answering many questions of the "who", "what", when" and "where" variety, and even, most impressively, in the last few centuries we are answering some of the "how" questions.

But we haven't answered any "why" questions and these questions don't yield to the scientific method, as normally applied. Historically, we have always tried to answer the "why" questions with religion.

All societies have had religions. Over time, societies evolve, and their religions go through a metamorphosis into higher level religious understandings. These new religious developments retain many features of the originals but sublimate the original myths into higher level metaphors that are more appropriate to the new requirements of civilization. However, the original spiritual myths were not untruths with which people deluded themselves; rather, they were best-effort theories to explain the world as they found it, like the best effort theories we use in science. When we find a better theory, we change our paradigm, but we still recognize the utility of the previous theory and paradigm, in its day, and the need for better theories and paradigms for the future.

To quote Thomas Nagel from his book *The Last Word* as he discusses scientific beliefs and theories:

"This means that most of our beliefs at any time must in some degree be regarded as provisional, since they may be replaced when a different balance of reasons is generated by new experience or theoretical ingenuity. It also means that an eternal set of rules of scientific method cannot be laid down in advance. But it does not mean that it cannot be true that a certain theory is the most reasonable to accept given the evidence available at a particular time, and it does not mean that the theory cannot be objectively true, however provisionally we may hold it. Truth is not the same as certainty, or universal acceptance."

Now, it is true that modern science is explaining more and more of the external world to us, and we certainly don't need religion to explain those things which science explains so well. We also don't need religious dogma, fundamentalism, fanaticism, intolerance, and exclusionary tactics. But we do need something to hold society together, which requires something more than materialism, technology, and economics; it requires a raison d'être, a spiritual glue to give civilization enough cohesion and meaning to make human life tolerable, meaningful, and fulfilling.

Physical science proceeds with the aid of physical measuring apparatus, but such tools are of little use in our quest to understand our inner sense of meaning and purpose. Yet our conscious awareness, our sense of our own free will and purposeful existence, is just as real a phenomenon as our awareness of the inputs from our senses. It is only the method of investigating and explicating that is, of necessity, a little different. Thus, the physical sciences, by their very definition and original axioms, only investigate and explicate the world available to our physical senses. It is no wonder then that the physical sciences do not explore meaning and purpose for which they can make no claims.

How do we investigate the reality of meaning and purpose? We do so by using the scientific method of proposing the most reasonable hypotheses, based on the best evidence available, and then subjecting these hypotheses to the most rigorous analyses and tests that we can devise.

We might propose our first hypothesis to be that existence has purpose and meaning. The alternate hypothesis can be that all of existence is accidental and utterly meaningless.

These hypotheses have more in common with the most basic axioms and hypotheses of physical science than may be apparent at first glance. Indeed, science itself seems to have originated out of the religious concept that the universe is orderly, obeys divine laws, and is thus comprehensible. The history of the discovery of deeper and deeper physical laws underpinning the physical universe confirms humanity's primordial religious instincts that the universe obeys laws and is thus comprehensible.

By using the principle of Occam's razor, the physical sciences advance by choosing the most simple, direct, and economical explanations. In other words, if a phenomenon can be explained by using only one axiom, or underlying physical law, then that is far preferable than an explanation of the same phenomenon using several axioms or principle laws.

By applying Occam's razor to the meaning and purpose of existence and consciousness, we see that it makes most sense to believe that existence is purposeful; this explains why the universe gave rise to human beings who have brains, which produce minds, which produce consciousness and awareness. By contrast, the other hypothesis must explain this whole evolution as a most improbable series of accidents that just happened to all lead to more and more intelligence and more and more order, in direct contradiction to the laws of thermodynamics.

To test our hypothesis that existence has meaning and purpose, we ask: does the evolutionary unfolding of the observable universe seem to proceed as if it had an underlying purpose? Indeed, the observable history of the universe is one of increasing complexity and then increasing intelligence, so much so that the physicists Brandon Carter, John D. Barrow, and Frank J. Tipler have proposed the Anthropic principle, which hypothesizes that the evolution of the universe unfolds such as to always increase intelligence, consciousness, and information processing. Indeed, this Anthropic principle, when analyzed, seems to hold true and also to pass the test of Occam's razor, in that no other hypothesis yet surmised seems to explain the unfolding of the evolution of the universe and life so economically.

The best minds of every society and culture that has ever existed all around the world have often come to surprisingly similar understandings about human existence and meaning. These ideas, which are known as the Perennial Philosophy, form the common underpinnings of almost every human religion that has ever existed. Even many of the best minds of modern science, including the discoverers of Quantum Physics and Relativity Theory, have expounded personal understandings of the philosophical basis of existence that are in accord with the Perennial Philosophy, including Albert Einstein, Werner Heisenberg, Erwin Schrodinger, Louis De Broglie, James Jeans, Max Planck, Wolfgang Pauli, and Arthur Eddington. An appeal to "authority" is not a "proof"; and I by no means mean to imply that these scientific giants believed that quantum physics and relativity "proved" the existence of God and purpose; but rather, that each of them found the concepts of spirit and purpose to be compatible with modern physics and appealing to the human understanding.

Religious truth is relative, theories are improved, new paradigms adopted. But we do have a choice, and we should choose to adopt those theories and paradigms that best fit the facts, best promote the common welfare, and offer the best vision of the future. Indeed, we need a common vision, common goals, and a community of meaning.

And our choices in these matters can be guided by reason, just as our scientific theories are. Karl Popper, the eminent theoretician of scientific method, has posited that in order to be a good scientific theory, a theory must be falsifiable. What this often means in a practical sense is that a scientific theory must be able to predict certain experimental outcomes which, if not forthcoming, would serve to falsify the theory itself. In religious terms, we can strive for an equivalent falsifiability of process. Where it is impossible to perform actual experiments on the entire history and future of the human race and the universe, we can instead observe the results that various processes have had in human affairs. One religious theory is not as good as the next; we do have a choice to make, and an important one. We should make a sound choice based on reason, evidence, and observation.

At the end of the day, there are two options. Either some underlying purpose or power designed things so conscious beings could evolve, or else we came about by a long series of complete accidents. But if we came about by accident, we should still devise core meanings and values and attempt to impose them on reality to the best of our ability. The long history of religion and art provide a solid basis on which to start.

Religion represents society's long-term memory and blueprints for the future. Some long-term memories are so important, have been so painfully won and at such a price, that they must never be forgotten. Most of all, we must have a common vision of the future, a vision that recognizes our need for more than just material comfort, and that represents the best possible aspirations of humanity. Most of our lives are spent on short-term affairs, duties, goals, and pursuits. Religion serves that noble function of supplying long-term guidance and direction, and momentum from generation to generation. As such, it is indispensable.

The Robot

I am a robot.

All I do is conditioned. I arise in the morning and go through my programmed activities and responses, exactly as I am wont to do. This is not from me; I function as an automaton.

But deep down inside, can I not find, underneath, a different self, an essence, from my childhood; perhaps seasoned, less naive, yet still open and fresh?

And cannot this deeper under-self yet receive some sort of heavenly aid? Some sort of aid from a source older than itself, higher and wiser, and more powerful? That aid so often spoken of, and felt as real presence deep within my soul and my spirit and my heart?

Boomers by the Waters of Babylon

Full Moon rising tonight, I feel like a werewolf, lost in space...

Please! STOP! Listen, hear me out! I'll be brief and to the point.

I remember Bob Dylan when he was young, singing beneath the starlight. I remember the Beatles, when they were young, I even remember the Rolling Stones. I remember when we all listened to the same songs, watched the same TV shows, dreamed the same dreams.

I remember running through the grass and trees on a summer night, laughing, playing, cousins all around. I remember green apples, Grandma's warnings, late night stories, and crickets croaking. I remember picnic summers, softball outings, and Friday night drive-ins.

I remember Willie Mays, center field grace, mothers' faces, school kids knowing the future was all before them, men on the moon, and the 60's swoon.

I recall being alive, so much to strive for.

I remember Abraham Lincoln. Honor, honesty, and destiny. Hard work, loyalty, failure, success, blood, guts, and civil war. I remember his dilemma, his courage, but mostly I remember his long, lanky humor on backwoods lawyer trips. Old Abe could make a day go by, and never miss a lick. He was ugly and homely and humble, and I miss old Abe.

Where did our present generation of politicians come from? Where are we going?

For God's sake, where did it all go, where did we go wrong? I'm going crazy here in the dark moonlight, screaming my brains out beneath the stars of fate. What in the hell is going on around here, anyway? When did we let the financial planners take over America, the stock selling shills on TV bombard our brains? When did money become the only savior, greed the only rule?

When did we decide to hate each other? Competition, hell, we got killing; you kill me, or I'll kill you. It's not the law of the jungle, it's worse than that; we got high tech tigers that kill for fun, or fear, or lust.

Are we going to just rot away as if nothing matters?

I want to build something; something that lasts. Something we all build, and grow, and sweat, and paint, and mend, and care for, and make, and stake our blood in the soil of America for future generations.

We got people dying all over the world. We got people hopeless, poor, powerless, and children lost and hungry. Poisoned air and water, ruined lives.

Excuse me, but we got souls exploding in thin air; blood is flowing, and nobody gives a damn.

I want Abe Lincoln back. I want our future back. If we don't have any money left after the crash, at least give us a future, a mission, a care, a matter, a soul to live for and die for. Give us back our heart and our country and our values and our spirit.

I remember how it was, the taste of life on our tongues. I want it back.

How does it feel, America, how does it feel?

A Boy, a Dog, and Quantum Uncertainty

"We are hanging in the balance of the reality of man, like every sparrow falling, like every grain of sand." —Bob Dylan

A boy was born in Cincinnati, Ohio, on October 19, 1952. As he grew, he looked around and noticed that he was born into a lower middle-class family that was less well off than many others. An early black and white TV set arrived in the family's apartment, and it showed him a world of upper middle-class people who had more money, more things, and more power. The boy suspected that people like this looked down on families like his, and he was jealous.

In addition to this, the boy was small and lacked strength, and he was timid. He had a sister only 11 months older than himself, and he was guilty of the sin of jealousy towards her also. He felt that the parents treated her like an adult and treated him like a child. Eventually, he noticed that the parents were very proudimmensely proud of her for being smart. The mother, in particular, took great pride in her learning to read at a young age. So, the boy eagerly began to learn to read from the daily newspaper and the family Bible. Once his sister began elementary school, the boy read her schoolbooks and tried to outdo her. Especially, he also learned some simple arithmetical tricks like multiplying by powers of ten, allowing him to pose simple multiplication questions and outdoing her in front of his parents. As the sister passed from grade to grade, he devoured all her schoolbooks at the beginning of each school year. Although the home had few books, he did have access to a public library and he eagerly read his mother's King James Bible, especially Genesis.

In short, he became an exceptionally good student and excelled in all standardized tests and made perfect grades in school. He succeeded far beyond his natural intelligence level, which was in fact only well within the normal range. It was not only a way to try to please his parents, but also the only way he saw to try to climb the social ladder and compete in the world beyond his family.

Of course, he eventually found out that there were many people much smarter than he, especially after he went away to university. But by being very diligent, opportunistic, and driven, he moved up. After college, he had a modicum of success in achieving the things people aspire to, such as money, status, and recognition. But it gradually dawned on him that these things, in and of themselves, were not satisfying. His life was being consumed by stress, worry and worldly cares. What would be left, at the end of his life, from all of these "accomplishments"?

And so, he began to search for underlying values. Maybe he should have put in more thought upfront, when he was younger, about what his life's goals should be. He began to read, study, and contemplate the great philosophical and religious traditions, questions, and books.

He particularly studied the world's major religious traditions and found meaning and beauty in all of them. In the end, his own native Christian tradition was most satisfying to him, but he also saw that there was a universal bedrock of values, traditions, mores, and beliefs that formed the foundation of all the world's civilizations. Whether you call it the Way, the Tao, the perennial philosophy, or the Golden Rule, it was an inherent understanding in all peoples, even when they sometimes actually behaved in diametrically opposite ways. In their hearts, in their consciences, all people knew right from wrong.

And it also dawned on him that there was no reason to agonize, worry, and fret about all these things. One could follow the Way of being a good Christian without losing the joy of everyday life by worrying about all the details of theological and philosophical niceties. He was certain that no one could ever be certain about such things anyway.

One problem though, having reached these sane, reasonable, and mature conclusions, was that the boy, now a man, looked at his hands, his arms, and his face in the mirror and saw the wrinkled skin of an old man. It was very late to take advantage of these moderate ideas and he had wasted much of his life with unwarranted and unnecessary concerns.

In thinking about all this, the old man began to consider how his beloved dog, Betsy, illustrated some good principles of how to enjoy life without over-thinking, and thus missing, some of life's best moments. When the family picked Betsy out of her litter, they chose her because, although she was the runt of the litter, she was the most outgoing and personable.

When the old man took Betsy on her daily walk, she would positively prance with joy. Everyone they met was captivated by her joie de vivre, her cute antics, and especially her personality. Betsy didn't walk, she positively danced with glee to be alive. She loved meeting all dogs and all people. When meeting an old friend, she would race in circles for an extended time, wagging her tail back and forth vigorously. Betsy wasn't the smartest dog, but she was cute, and she knew it. She enjoyed life. In her ineffable dogness, she knew that she was lucky the family picked her, lucky they kept her, and lucky to be alive.

The old man learned from Betsy the lesson to enjoy life, not overthink or worry about the details, and to cherish the day-to-day happiness of being. But still, he thought, there is a difference between dogs and people. People can decide, plan, make things happen, make a difference, and do good or evil. And even as much as Betsy loved everyone and everything, people can and do love in a more profound way. The old man, eager to take advantage of the insights he learned from Betsy, still wanted to know what makes people different, and why people sometimes must suffer so. Why was the carefree life of a dog inappropriate for a person? Why did Socrates say that "the unexamined life is not worth living?"

And so, he asked himself: can modern science shed any light on these questions? Perhaps the leading scientific theory and paradigm of our time is quantum physics. There are several mathematical ways to express quantum physics, but all lead to the same results and predictions. And all of them contain an element of chance, or rather, they precisely and definitively predict the actual results that will occur at atomic levels, but only in a statistical way. The statistical probabilities that quantum physics predicts always hold true, but in any given iso-lated incident, it is impossible to say exactly what will occur, only that in many incidents of a particular kind, the results will obey the sta-tistical probabilities predicted by quantum physics. Some outcomes may be, depending on the conditions and circumstances, very likely to occur; and other outcomes may be very unlikely to occur.

So, the laws of the universe spell out precisely how the universe will evolve, on a large scale in the future; but the short-term details will vary because of the statistical nature of individual quantum phenom-ena. Some actions are more likely, some less so, and on average over time the equations are never violated. But still, in any individual in-stance, a seemingly random or chance factor exists, prompting Ein-stein, who disliked this aspect of quantum physics and felt that it must be wrong, to remark that "God doesn't play dice with the universe".

One may hypothesize that God created the quantum systems that we can describe using the quantum field equations, with all their long-term exactness and precision, in order to give certain long-term ten-dencies and outcomes, but S/He reserved certain controls. Thus, every quantum event, interaction, and outcome always follows the quan-tum field equations, but God reserves the ability and responsibility to decide to use the "chance" part of any atomic event to affect out-comes. Thus, God is restricted to maintaining the long-term statis-tical tendencies required by the equations, but S/He can manipulate the "chance" variation to affect short term individual outcomes. Thus, God created a law-abiding system with long-term ramifications, but can still "interfere" on a quantum level to a certain extent. In effect, God would be controlling when and where the statistically rare events would occur.

This could allow God to perform what we would perceive as physical miracles on a macroscopic scale, in very rare instances, while maintaining a law-abiding universe. God is a law maker, not a law breaker.

But where do people fit into all of this? Well, God is said to have made people in Their own image. Maybe this means that S/He gave people at least a small ability to also affect how Creation turns out. If God can choose, at least in rare circumstances, to affect how the statistical predictions of quantum physics play out, maybe S/He gave people a small bit of ability to affect reality also. For instance, one might hypothesize at least three ways this could happen. First, people, by the very act of measuring atomic events and performing experiments, could be partially causing certain outcomes. Secondly, people often pray to God to help in various circumstances, and maybe God sometimes listens to those prayers and, on occasion, intervenes at the atomic level in ways that might even have macroscopic effects. Thirdly, people plan, think, hypothesize, and act in purposeful ways, thus affecting how the world evolves over time. People are meaning-making creatures.

Thus, God created people with free will to do, to decide, to be, and to create. In a sense, God sacrificed total control by allowing humans the freedom to create, decide, do, and affect outcomes. In fact, sacrificing and suffering, in order to create better outcomes, seem to be core parts of God's attributes. After all, God gave Their only begotten Son to be sacrificed by crucifixion. Jesus suffered, and He sacrificed Himself, and He even exhibited humility. We don't normally consider these things to be core attributes of God, but on the other hand, Jesus shows us what God is like. When we look at Jesus, we see what God is like. And Jesus suffered and was sacrificed, so hypothetically, God values and somehow exhibits these attributes.

And so God made suffering and sacrifice part of the human condi-
tion. This is hard for us to accept. But it may be a necessary part of
how we are to co-create the future, working together with God, mak-
ing short-term sacrifices, and sometimes suffering a lot, but helping
to create greater things.

Another Way

Once upon a time there was a flock of birds. This particular flock of birds was quite large and had been inspired by the Most Wondrous Bird of all time, a Bird so lustrous that all birds agreed to follow it on a quest of utmost beauty and importance.

After a while, the Most Wondrous Bird passed on, but left a magical Song with so many wondrous melodies that all who heard it were enchanted. Some individual birds only heard and understood one particular melody; other birds caught on to a different melody. Each bird remembered enough fragments of a melody to be enchanted for life and to follow the flock on the quest, but no one recalled all the melodies, for the Great Melody was infinite and varied. But only with all the many melodies sung together could the flock be truly guided to reach the ultimate goal of the vision-quest, a Paradise at the end of a long torturous series of dangerous valleys between horrible mountain peaks with awful predators. Worse, the mountains each beckoned with sidetracks and dead ends which led not to Paradise, but to discordant valleys of disunity, for only small fragments of the flock could follow any given sidetrack.

The birds were in a big hurry and started out. As the flock flew between two towering and scary mountains, a fight broke out. One bird remembered perfectly well that they were supposed to go left; another cited the Song as saying they had to go right; both were sure they were right, so soon the group was about to split up, as each bird was determined to follow the Melody and magical lyrics as it understood them.

"We must break up this group," one said. "It is too divergent and discordant. Surely the Most Wondrous Bird could not have inspired all of us. We are too different. If my Melody is right and giving us correct guidance, as I'm 100% sure it is, then some of these other birds are wrong in their memories, and in fact some of their songs sound like pure evil, not beauty and truth."

But another bird spoke up and barely managed to carry the day, at least for many of them. "If we split up, we will lose the guidance of the Song," she said. "We must stay together." To herself she said "I'm sure some of these birds are dead wrong, but they will be straightened out when we reach paradise valley, and they hear the whole melody again all together. Even though they are wrong, and if left alone would corrupt the Great Song, we will keep them together unless they stray too far."

And yet, some birds split off into side groups and went their separate ways.

And so, the main group set out. One after another, strange birds took the lead of the ragged band for short intervals. While feeling insane for following some of these weird birds, the individual birds flew wearily on. Each mountain pass provided a fresh opportunity to choose the wrong route. It was a mottled crew, to be sure, but somehow, they weaved in and out amidst the towering and forbidding mountains.

After a long while, however, the battered flock was at the point of exhaustion and individual birds began to have nervous breakdowns. "I'd better leave and fly on my own, for better to abandon even the Most Great Song than to suffer a nervous breakdown. Besides, this flock has no chance at all of ever finding the whole Melody again anyway," said more than one bird to itself.

And then it happened. Slowly, a beautiful but translucent bird began to appear in front of the flock. With each beat of the little birds' wings, the big, beautiful bird became more visible to the naked eye. As they rounded a corner between two awesome mountains, some other lost sub-flocks came into view.

Each flock was led by a Translucent Bird of Unity, and upon making formation together in the large valley, they all became a flock of the most beautiful birds ever seen. And right then all the birds heard, for the first time in thousands of years, the Whole Song, which told of the Beautiful Translucent Bird of Unity and how it would lead them to the promised land.

Each sub-melody told of the need for all the individual birds' tunes, even with their idiosyncrasies and imperfections, and how they would be led by a Transparent Bird of Unity until they were all brought together in the Valley of Paradise. If they had all parted ways back there, they could all have become lost forever in the valleys of despair. But they were always led by a Transparent Bird of Unity, even when they squabbled and fought. But they didn't know it, because they couldn't see it.

The key was to listen to each bird's point of view, even though it was naturally strange and discordant. After all, each little bird had only a small fragment of the original and final Song.

"There is Another Way," sang the now visible Bird of Unity, "to listen to each other, even when it's ugly, so that later you can hear the entire melodious symphony which can only be sung by the whole flock. The path was only right when each bird's small part was sung, so no bird could have made it to this sweet valley unless all birds came together."

From then on, the flock of wild birds flew over the broad valley, each sub-flock swerving wildly, but the whole flock guided unerringly by the beautiful Bird of Unity.

Miracles

Do miracles happen? Are any reported miracles real, or are they all merely artifacts of gullibility, wishful thinking, and fraud? I propose that some miracles do happen and are real, but that God uses natural laws to accomplish miracles, because God is a law maker, not a law breaker.

How does God use natural laws to accomplish divine purposes? Let us start with quantum physics, the most basic and important natural laws undergirding our current understanding of physical reality. Quantum field theory accurately describes and predicts without fail, but it involves statistics and probability. In any situation, quantum field theory predicts what will happen in an accurate statistical way, with various outcomes having different probabilities. Einstein said, "God doesn't play dice with the universe", but in a sense God does play dice. The outcomes precisely and infallibly follow the predictions of quantum field theory, with the individual occurrences following the predicted probabilities and distributions, but when each possible outcome occurs being governed by purely random chance. But maybe God is, at least some of the time, involved in deciding and determining which statistically possible outcome occurs when. Maybe God, in some cases, chooses statistically very unlikely outcomes of quantum events, to cause what to us seem to be miracles. In the long term, the quantum field equations play out as expected, but statistically unlikely events occur when God so decides. Perhaps chance is the subtle left hand of God.

Some even hypothesize a theory of panpsychism, in which the smallest possible units of quantum "nodes" of reality exhibit minuscule quanta of consciousness that could influence the statistical outcomes of quantum events. But however you slice it, the statistical nature of quantum reality opens the door to even extremely unlikely events happening extremely rarely. Our kind of science is very good at studying, describing, and predicting repetitive phenomena, but not so good at studying, describing, and predicting non-repeating, very rare and even unique phenomena. It is even possible that the quantum field equations, along with their initial conditions, set up one or more truly unique events, baked into the future from the very beginning.

Another factor that can influence miracles is psychology. The human mind is a complex, powerful thing. Certainly, the well-known placebo effect demonstrates that the mind can cause very real beneficial changes to the physical body. The implications of this for faith healing are obvious. When a charismatic, trusted healer prays for or lays on hands to heal a person, that person's mind may well initiate powerful, helpful processes in the body, in a sort of reverse psychosomatic effect. Group psychology may also help foster surprising outcomes, for instance the collective spirit, energy, and drive of Jesus' apostles in spreading the growth of Christianity.

God also helps those who help themselves. Most important outcomes are over-determined, and by that, I mean that the outcome is driven by more than one important reason behind it. As a possible example, consider Moses's parting of the Reed Sea during the Exodus. God may well have influenced quantum events to contribute to this event, but perhaps also Moses and the other Israelite leaders were well informed, smart, and decisive. They may have known that there was an underwater land bridge in a particular spot in the Reed Sea[1], and that the waters shallowly covering the land bridge were likely to be at minimum at a particular time due to winds and waves, so they timed the crossing such that the Egyptians, with their heavy chariots, would become stuck in the mud and destroyed by rising water.

Also, Moses may have used his extensive knowledge of the Sinai desert in order to utilize a natural phenomenon to solve the enormous logistical challenge of feeding the Hebrews. Dr. F.S. Bodenheimer, of Hebrew University in Jerusalem, proposed that the manna consisted of honeydew-like excretions of certain insects which feed on the tamarisk tree. The drops of this excretion solidify in the hot desert air. Even today, locals make confections from this material. If these drops were gathered in the early morning, they could be baked into palatable cakes. As is described in the book of Exodus, if the manna is not gathered until later in the day, insects consume it. So maybe Moses used information and smarts to help feed the people. But chance, or God, had to cooperate to make the manna available in sufficient quantity at just the right time and place.

---

1   A literal translation of the biblical passage is "Sea of Reeds", and although this has usually been translated as "Red Sea", many scholars believe the crossing to have occurred to the north in the shallower isthmus of the Gulf of Suez sometimes referred to as the "Sea of Reeds".

So, in ways like these, over a long period of time from Abraham to Moses through the later prophets to Jesus, the Israelites' faith in a supreme monotheistic God could have been a valid process guided by divine providence and human reason, but without direct "magical" suspension of natural physical laws. For instance, Jesus' healings could have been a valid process guided by divine providence and utilizing psychological factors. Intriguingly, Jesus is quoted as saying that He could work no wonders in certain Galilean regions because of the lack of faith of the inhabitants.

Then we come to the most outstanding miracle of all times, the resurrection. It is a mystery because we don't have all the detailed facts, and it is impossible to "prove" what happened. But something happened, and there are two major aspects to what was reported. First, we have the empty tomb. Second, we have the appearances to the apostles and others, including the appearance to Paul on the road to Damascus. While there have been reports in many places and times of deceased persons making appearances, none have had the impact that Jesus has had. Curiously, the empty tomb is rarer. I have been unable to find many stories of empty tombs. I am sure such stories must have been told, but they don't seem to be common. Of course, it is not impossible that all the stories about Jesus are exaggerations, misunderstandings, etc. But that is not the only possibility. The combination of the empty tomb, the post resurrection appearances, and the impact on the apostles and human history are without a doubt unique and uniquely important. It is frustrating that we don't have definitive exact proof. But in a sense, proof of such a happening is simply not possible. Even if the entire crucifixion, burial, resurrection, and subsequent appearances had been filmed, we could hypothesize that the film was doctored, altered, or otherwise made fake. Proof is not possible. Such a unique and important event depends on how we approach it and understand it. The most pivotal hinge in human history is enigmatic, mysterious, and consequential.

But we do have the reports that were written a few decades after the events. These reports in the Gospels and the letters of Paul are extraordinary documents that make it clear that the apostles really believed that there was an empty tomb and that a resurrected Jesus subsequently appeared to them. How we understand and interpret their reports is an open question, but I have no doubt that they believed in them.

And if we are looking for proof of miracles, it exists. Consider the very real miracles of the existence of the universe, life, human beings, and consciousness. Even from a scientific point of view, the laws of nature and the initial conditions of the universe would have had to be so finely tuned to allow anything to exist, especially life, to be all but impossible. To believe that all this happened by blind luck and for no reason would be illogical. It is infinitely more rational to believe that all that is has a cause and meaning, than to believe it is a mathematically impossible accident.

When you lay down to go to sleep, contemplate the complex beauty of the universe, our planet, nature, life, and human society, and it will gladden your heart and create joy and wonder, no matter your circumstances. You can go from rags to riches in the silence of the night.

Unity

In the Gospel of Mark, Jesus said "who isn't against us is for us". However, the Gospel of John reports Him to have said "do not think that I came to bring peace on earth. I did not come to bring peace but a sword." So, let's face it, it is complicated. But undeniably, Christianity and other religions have been fraught with divisions, arguments, and fighting. In Russia in the 1600's, a great schism occurred based partly on whether the sign of the cross should be made with two fingers or three. Tens of thousands of people died. In 1066, Christianity split into Eastern Orthodox and Catholic segments, partly because of three additional words added to the Nicene Creed. The Nicene Creed itself was created in the fourth century in response to many bitter disputes over theology. The Protestant Reformation resulted in wars killing millions of people. And don't overlook the many wars and dead in the centuries-long conflicts between Sunni and Shia Muslims. One is tempted to remark that if people are going to fight wars over religion, they would be better off without religion.

But surely, we would be better off to focus on what we have in common. Religions differ in myriad ways in theology, dogma, and doctrine, but most major religions have a great deal in common in terms of morality and ethics. Jesus emphasized love for God and love for one's fellow humans over and above doctrinal and ritualistic details. Surely, all Christians can agree with Jesus that these are the two greatest commandments. And almost all major religions have a version of the Golden Rule: "do unto others as you would have them do unto you". We should love and honor all who those who heed the two great commandments by recognizing that life has Purpose and Meaning and acknowledging the Golden Rule and the primacy of love for one's fellow humans.

In a lifetime of searching, I have found the life and teachings of Jesus to be my best clues as to what is right and good. Jesus incarnated in a particular time and place. If He were here physically today, I doubt He would approve of religious strife and hatred, and I suspect that He would love people of all religions.

Consider prayer, which is another universal amongst major world religions. As a Christian, I can attest that prayer works. It calms and focuses the mind, improves the mood, and promotes optimism. Ultimately, through the subtle left hand of God, it often improves outcomes. Once, in Ahmedabad in Gujarat Province of India, I happened to walk by a courtyard full of sincere, reverent, and devoted ladies of the Jain faith. Their piety moved me, and I was struck by their indistinguishability from reverent Christian groups I have seen and participated with. I have seen similar scenes at Shinto shrines in Japan, Buddhist temples in China, Japan, and the United States, and at an Ismaili Mosque in the USA. I think the same God is listening to all these prayers, at least at some level and in some sense. I also have read prayers from both ancient Egypt and Sumer (circa 4,000 years ago) that would fit into the biblical book of Psalms or one of the Hebrew prophets' books without attracting notice. Prayer is truly universal.

Peace be unto all people of good will.

Per Baha'u'llah, "the earth is but one country, and mankind its citizens."

Confucius

The modern age could do worse than to revisit and emulate the sage Confucius, who in around 500 BC searched, researched, and rescued the very best elements of Chinese civilization and lived and taught these precepts. He set an example that was emulated by his disciples and subsequently taught for the next 2,500 years, forming a bedrock of Chinese civilization. Confucius did not want to create anything new, but rather identify, collate, and pass on the best of the ancient ethics, morals, rituals, behaviors, and principles of the past. He did not much concern himself with gods, theology, or religious dogma, but rather with the practical elements of living a good life. He taught his version of the Golden Rule, "What you do not wish for yourself, do not do to others." He also expressed this as "Never impose on others what you would not choose for yourself." He respected all the ancient religious traditions and focused on the five cardinal virtues: benevolence, righteousness, propriety, wisdom, and fidelity. He prized study, knowledge, and learning, along with music and poetry. Most of all, he cherished and valued the core traditions that had stood the test of time and produced good results.

What if we applied Confucius' methods today? What if we surveyed
the vastly larger set of the best traditions of humanity available to us
now? We could use the core ethical, moral, and philosophical learnings
of all the world's religious traditions, including Judaism, Christianity,
Islam, Zoroastrianism, Hinduism, Buddhism, Sikhism, Jainism, Tao-
ism, Shinto, the Baha'i Faith, and others. Though the specific dogmas,
theologies, and mythologies may vary, the core ethical principles are
similar. One might choose to live according to the specific traditions
of one particular religion, but still respect the learning, virtue, and
sacredness of all other religions, traditions, sages, and prophets. Or, if
one could not accept any specific religion, one could still embrace the
ethical and spiritual core of all of them. In China, an updated Confu-
cianism backed up by a broad-minded perennial philosophy might be
a good religion with Chinese characteristics.

God of Abraham

Abraham re-thought what God is. He accepted all that was good from the religions of the Near East, starting with Sumerian religion, but also including aspects of Semitic and Egyptian religion. But he removed all aspects of their religious practices that involved acts that his conscience decided were evil, most prominently being child sacrifice. This was a big step. He strongly believed that God revealed to him that he should sacrifice his most beloved son, and this was consistent with widespread practice and belief in his culture. But somewhere deep within him, he felt it was wrong and then "an angel" revealed to him that he should not sacrifice his son but sacrifice a ram instead. That required Abraham to decide whether to follow the dictates of this angel or the previous dictate that he believed came directly from God. He followed the angel's instructions. This is an important principle: If ever God "tells" us to do something that egregiously violates our conscience, we should know that the evil direction was not from God. God gave us consciences to use.

And this critical incident of Abraham and Isaac builds upon a principle that Abraham used in re-conceiving what God is like. Abraham intuited that God is all good, and there is no evil or imperfection in God. Abraham argued with God about the morality of destroying all inhabitants of Sodom and Gomorrah. He also decided that no particular part of Creation could represent God, because God was Creator of all Creation. Every part of Creation is good, but God is greater than any part, and God didn't need any helper gods or subordinate gods.

Bottom line, Abraham began to see God as the truth and reality of a divine Purpose beyond all contingent facts, beyond humanity's understanding, and beyond Creation. He trusted that God always has the greater good in mind, and always champions justice, and that all apparent evil and "bad things happening to good people" would ultimately be resolved in favor of the greater good. He saw that encumbering his understanding of God with unnecessary baggage, whether images, representations, or gods of forces and aspects of nature, were beneath the true dignity of the true God. Abraham believed in God, but he didn't believe anymore in all the specific dogmas of his culture's previous religious traditions, if those specific beliefs violated the understanding of God as a pure, all powerful, and all good monotheistic God.

But Abraham did not throw out the baby with the bathwater. He kept and maintained the good things from previous religious practices, especially all emphases on doing good. He also kept some ritual practices. He set up altars to God and performed animal sacrifices. He honored the religious practices of others when they did not violate his new understandings. For instance, he honored Melchizedek and participated in Melchizedek's worship of El, the High God in many middle eastern traditions. Most importantly, Abraham recognized the importance of worship, prayer, ethics, and morality.

He also established, or continued, other practices to distinguish and maintain unity among his new faith community, such as circumcision. These kinds of practices may not be crucial to any ethical standard, but are sometimes useful in community building and maintenance.

The history of the Abrahamic religions has, at least to some extent, built upon and further refined this focus on a monotheistic, all good God. But perhaps there is further to go. All the Abrahamic religions have in common a belief in an all-powerful, all good, purposeful God that can be trusted to lead all beings to the ultimate good, and that it is the duty of humans to try to imitate the goodness of God. Maybe that is more important than any specific differences in dogmatic beliefs.

We could do worse than to worship the God of Abraham. But we need to respect and honor other religious traditions, and we need to practice spiritual disciplines that involve gratitude, awe, devotion, and a firm commitment to ethics and morality. These virtuous activities can be found in any of the Abrahamic religions, and in many other religions that recognize something like the Golden Rule.

In my case, Christianity is the Way, because I recognize Jesus as the ultimate Exemplar of God and as our Savior. But all who practice moral religions should cherish the wider community of good religious beliefs in the world.

The God of Abraham is a transcendent First Mover and Sustainer Who is all loving and all demanding. How would Abraham apply his conception of God to today's situation, given an additional 4,000 years of human history and experience?

Yin-Yang, the 51% Solution

We are living on a knife's edge.

Which way we will go is uncertain.

Consider how it is that anything exists at all. The only reason that atoms, stars, and galaxies can exist is because the physical constants of nature are fine-tuned to a razor's edge. And on top of that, the physical constants are even more micro-tuned to allow life to emerge; much less intelligent, conscious life.

So, given the miracle of our existence, we look around to see that the physical world appears to be meaningless, with no sign of caring or purpose. But who can dispute the beauty of the universe, earth's biosphere, and human love and ingenuity?

In fact, the beauty and pain of our existence are nearly balanced; they appear to carry surprisingly similar weights.

While any individual person may experience more than her share of horror and pain, another individual may experience love, joy, and harmony. What do we make of this? What will tip the scales?

It seems to me that the only variable is the human capacity for conscious choice, coupled with human feelings for moral and ethical values, along with rational evaluation.

In a world so closely balanced between good and evil, so finely tuned between opposites, what else can tip the scales? Even if you extend the capability for conscious, ethical choice to some other animals (whales, dolphins, primates, elephants, crows?) or even hypothetical alien life forms, the basic argument stays the same.

We are conscious, moral agents poised to help tip the balance one way or the other.

Consider within human society and history how so many key variables have been poised between good and evil. Has religion been more good or more evil, on balance, over human history? Have humans been loving and kind, or cruel and evil?

No matter how meager our powers, no matter how limited our options, no matter how balanced our propensities for good and evil, we carry the ability to tip the balance of human activities one way or the other. Given the precarious knife's edge on which the universe teeters, we have the ability to move the needle to perhaps 50.001% good, versus 49.999% evil.

So, no matter how much evil my sinful self may harbor, I choose to strive to do more good than evil, even if it is by a small amount. So should we all strive to tip the balance towards the 51% goal.

I choose to believe in and to pursue a world with more good than evil, with more purpose than nihilism, and with more beauty than pain. Why we are poised on such a precarious and unlikely cliff I do not know; but I recognize the possibilities, the importance, and the moral imperative of positive choice, decisive action, and unlikely faith.

Light

In the very beginning of the very first book of the ancient Hebrew Torah, in the first creative act, God said "Let there be light."

Light is made up of electromagnetic waves. We know what electricity is, even if it's just from sparks caused by static electricity and lightning. We also know what magnets do. How strange and wonderful that "waves" combining these two (related) kinds of energy can manifest as visible light. Each electromagnetic wave has a frequency of vibration and an associated wavelength. The higher the frequency, the shorter the wavelength. We can see electromagnetic waves in a certain frequency range, with each specific frequency being perceived as different in color, from red (the lowest frequency and longest wavelength we can see) through all the colors of the rainbow up to violet, the highest frequency we can see. Beyond that are invisible ultraviolet waves: X Rays and gamma rays. Below the frequency of the color red, are infrared waves and radio waves.

Electromagnetic waves are important. The speed of electromagnetic waves is a constant and defines the fastest speed at which anything can move. Nothing is more crucial to understanding the physical universe than electromagnetic waves. But electromagnetism can also behave as particles. The smallest quantum of electromagnetism possible is called a photon. Photons are massless particles and move at the speed of light. Normal physical objects, such as electrons or protons or human beings, can approach the speed of light, but never quite get there; as they speed up, their mass increases, they become heavier, and at the speed of light their mass would become infinite. Another oddity is that, as matter moves faster, time slows down, and at the actual speed of light, the passage of time would stop. Light, (or any electromagnetic wave), can and does travel at the speed of light because it has no mass to become infinite. If a photon could perceive the passage of time, it would perceive that it took no time at all for it to travel across the entire width of the universe; it would seem to itself that it crossed the entire universe instantaneously.

To a photon, everything is everywhere, and every time is now.

How miraculous is light! Many religious traditions describe God as being light-like. In the Bible, God created light first, and God is described by using light as a metaphor. God's face shines so bright that no man sees Their face and lives. In many near-death experiences, people see the Light of God, and often see new colors of light.

The human brain creates electromagnetic waves, and these waves radiate out into space. These do decrease in strength as time passes and they dissipate into space, but they are never actually completely destroyed. Perhaps remnants of these electromagnetic waves persist. Quantum processes in the brain also leave their marks, which—like all energetic phenomenon—are never destroyed. The Penrose-Hameroff theory hypothesizes that our consciousness itself arises from quantum processes in the brain.

Like scratches on wet clay, hardened in the sun, the records of our existence are faint but eternal.

Electromagnetic Waves

The human brain creates electromagnetic vibrations and waves which radiate out from the skull into the surrounding space. A transceiver could be devised that would be able to receive and decode these messages and transmit like messages to another human. Indeed, two humans so equipped could communicate directly brain to brain. A whole earth of such humans could tune into a planet-wide symphony of celestial music.

It is readily apparent that electromagnetic waves such as these are not destroyed by distance or time; their effects are eternal. Not only could they be used to communicate over long distances between stars and galaxies, but they will remain until the final Omega Point of the universe billions of years from now; we truly are immortal, to the extent that we think.

The electromagnetic waves produced by our brains do not exist in isolation. The frequencies, sequences, durations, and rhythms of each individual brain are superimposed on each other. The total effects are so complex that they can only be likened to music; it is musical sequences of frequency, timing, and rhythm that represent the most complex patterns that the human mind can hold in attention at any given moment.

The brainwaves of one individual overlap with another's, with complex feedback loops affected by partial synchronizations caused by language, religion, love, and innumerable other human commonalities. These feedback patterns extend to the ends of the universe, no matter how faint, world without end.

Music and song were early achievements of the human brain, leading indicators of the brain's future powers that initiated feedback loops, fostering both the necessity and the means for further intellectual development.

It is both appropriate and beautiful that music and song, which to us perhaps appear to be vestigial capabilities with no more utility than the appendix, are, in reality, the mainspring of our past intellectual triumphs and pivotal to our future destiny.

Without the capability to hold in mind complex sequences of frequencies and rhythms, our species would never have been able to learn language and other complex mental phenomena. Without these same musical capabilities which allow us to hold in mind multiple perspectives on time, space, and pattern recognition, we would never be able to learn to produce the intimately detailed and resonant feedback loops necessary for the future intellectual destiny of the multiverse.

It's all a matter of timing...

Vision Logic

Each moment, each world divides into an infinite number of worlds. Each decision you make is important and creates a new quantum mechanical universe. Sure, some versions of the new worlds may contain versions of you that chose differently.

But when you stand back and look at all the multiplying worlds from a non-temporal vantage point, certain symmetries emerge. Patterns of informational consonance, morale awareness, and circumstantial similarities and structures radiate before us like stars shining light in an infinite number of directions from fixed points.

So, when a conscious individual human dies, he ceases to exist in his own temporal world (which is only one of the infinitely graded versions of himself across worlds) and from a temporal, linear point of view, his brain is gone and no thinking across time continues to exist.

But from a non-temporal vantage point, the effects of his choices and those of the many versions of himself not only exist, but they radiate outwards from each decision point in a complex, crystal-like structure of immense significance.

So, we have before us a complex symphony of resonant structures. While we cannot fully understand these non-temporal structures, we can certainly not say that they don't exist. Therefore, conscious life is, in important ways, non-temporal and eternal.

Consciousness Revisited

Deep within everyone, there exists a consciousness free of ego, separateness, and death.

When you think of "yourself", you may think of your inner dialogue, your verbal thoughts that begin with the word "I". But who is this "I" in your head?

This "I" cannot be the real inner you, because your mind is forming the thought which results in a sentence beginning with the word "I".

Ask this question of the "I" in your mind: "Who are you, I am waiting for an answer". But do not form the "answer" yourself, using your ego and mental verbal machinery; instead, listen carefully for the answer from deep within.

You will hear no words, if you do this experiment carefully. Instead, you will experience a timeless center of being, a deep well of mind. From deep below the surface, the wordless joy of existence will swell up from within and you will know the peace of glimpsing your real existence, your timeless reality.

This reality of existence is shared by all humans, of whatever race, geographic location, and time. You can share in their joy, experience, and triumph, but you also must share in their pain and suffering.

All sentient beings share in this eternal ground of being to the extent that their nature allows. But human beings are at a very high level of conscious existence, and their spiritual reality is precious indeed. We all must honor and cherish this shared dignity and reality of humanity.

So, this is the basis for moral and ethical behavior, as well as religious experience. Once we realize our inner connection with all living beings, and especially with all human spirits, then we can no longer behave as if only our own limited wellbeing matters. What matters is the reality of all living souls. Therefore, morals do matter.

Whatever situation you are in, try to experience the inner reality of the consciousness of all humans present and involved. Experienced from this viewpoint, a peaceful and much more level-headed consciousness within yourself can and will better evaluate the true ramifications of all actions, decisions, and interactions within the group.

Try this experiment: when sitting or standing in a group of people, think about your own inner reality, that point of infinite consciousness deep within you, far beyond your own fragile ego. Now, consider each of the other people in your group as similar infinite points of consciousness. Realize the inter-connectedness of all these points of consciousness. Now relate to the group as the magnificent congress of souls that it really is! You will affect great changes for the better in your happiness, well-being, and wisdom in group dealings.

Time and Mind

Close your eyes. Imagine a time before anything existed. Nothing exists. No things, no minds, no ideas, no God, no space, no time, no anything. Is the absence of anything something? Is it possible that from nothing, came what we have now? Or does the very concept of existence imply that existence was always possible?

If you allow your mind to meditate on this, you will realize that the existence of things, including the universe, is completely irrelevant unless the mind and consciousness exist. Without mind, there is no difference between utter nothingness and a complete physical universe. Mind is all that matters.

Therefore, the current existence of the mind, as proven to yourself by your own thoughts and meditation on this theme, may have important implications. If death is utter annihilation of mind, and all things ultimately die, then we would go into nothingness, and that nothingness would be as if nothing had ever existed. Yet something exists now.

I leave it to you. Does the existence of your own mind right now imply that mind has always existed and always will exist? If the mind is the ultimate stuff of the universe, how can mind cease to exist? Is it more reasonable to believe in the primacy and staying power of mind, or of the physical universe?

Something is primary about mind. How does the mind relate to time? Think about the very beginning of the universe. Think about the very beginning of mind. Think about the end of the universe, and the end of mind. Does the mind die? If the mind is as important as it appears to be, what does your mind tell you about these subjects, when meditating most deeply?

God the Preserver

God sees, knows, and preserves all good things. Every good thought, deed, and quality is preserved for all time. That which is dross is rejected and dies. All is weighed in the scales of justice.

So, every good thing about you will be preserved for all time by God. Every good thought, action, and quality will be preserved. Your bad and worthless thoughts, actions, and qualities will not be preserved; they will die for all eternity. Even Hitler must have had some good qualities, however few. But saints have more.

Do you want to live forever? What about you is worth living? Should you choose actions, thoughts and deeds that are worthy of life?

The ancient Egyptians believed in an afterlife review in which a deceased person was weighed on the scales of life. The Bible talks of sinners being burned in everlasting fire and annihilation, and of saints rejoicing in a perfect heaven of eternal life. Perhaps parts of us will experience each?

Think Big

The God Concept

What do we mean by the use of the word "God"? The word has been used for so long, and in so many ways, that it is difficult to encompass. Some have argued that it has been used and misused in so many ways as to become meaningless and obsolete. Do we all have different ideas and connotations when we think about the meaning of the word "God"? Are there other words which might be more serviceable in describing the divine? Is the word a sort of empty set?

On the contrary, I believe that the concept of God represents, in an admirably data-compressed way, the highest goals, ideas, and aspirations of humanity. The God concept represents the ultimate goals of transcendence, of reaching beyond, of striving for the true meanings of human existence. If God did not exist, we would be left muddling around in the muck of meaningless, goal-less, hopeless nihilism. God represents the ultimate beyond; that which our hearts and our innermost minds whisper to us in our dreams at night; that which we secretly know is true, even though we know equally well that we cannot comprehend it, cannot encompass it, cannot intellectually approach it with our limited linguistic skills. God is beyond any human language, but S/He whispers to our hearts in the still of the night.

God represents the most noble idea or meme of which humans are capable. It is the glory of humankind to be able to even sense the presence of the divine. Without the sense of the divine which lies entirely beyond our capabilities, we would be the most limited of creatures. To be blessed with rational thought, consciousness, and self-awareness, but denied the aspirations of following the God concept, would leave us limited, proscribed from the reality which would make our awareness meaningful.

God is unknowable, completely. S/He is, however, the lodestar of our existence, our minds, and our inspiration.

The potential to recognize the God concept is somehow built into our mental machinery by the genetic records in our evolutionary history. And I believe that the fact that so noble a concept is hard- or soft-wired into our mental makeup is magnificent, and ultimately true. For evolution does not build in such complex designs and concepts unless there is a reality about them, and a utility. I believe that in some mysterious and unknown way, the necessity to evolve a mental mechanism for such an ultimately true concept, such a foundational concept as the God concept, was somehow necessary in the evolutionary creation of high intelligence and the human ability to survive, to create, and even to transcend.

So, I believe that we have an inherent religious instinct in human nature that repeatedly expresses itself in human cultures. I believe that religious instinct has positive survival value and pragmatic benefits. There is no downside to striving high.

I believe the inbuilt religious instinct, which leads to our ability to formulate the God concept, ultimately forms the basis for our ability to have morality. Thus, it is essential to our very humanity.

If dogs and other social animals instinctually form natural hierarchies, with an alpha dog emerging as the leader of the pack, then who is to lead the human social pack? It is better to be led by a transcendent God concept in the sky, or ultimately in another and better world, than to be led by individual egotistical humans.

Amongst humans, there is no Other, except that Other Who positively transcends everything which we can know, feel, and be. Yes, we are better off to think big, not small, and to follow the best lights of the God concept into the transcendent future.

And so, my dear readers, when you set out to build something, think big. Build big. For humanity is not placed on this earth and in this universe to accomplish small tasks, nor to build small concepts, structures, and organizations. A humanity that can conceive of God should dream big dreams, and then see them through to reality.

God will be what God will be. We will be what we will become. In some mysterious way, the two are intertwined.

Prayer

Oh my God, I pray to you.

What have I wrought?

Have mercy on me and my soul and on all sentient creatures.

I come to this dark night of the soul knowing nothing, except that I don't know how to deal with what's going on in my life.

I know not anything, nor can I discern your wishes. I pray that you guide and teach us.

I choose to accept Jesus Christ as my personal savior and as the savior of the world. May His will be done.

I do not dishonor or devalue any religious tradition. I see great value in all the world's major religious traditions. I believe religions add immensely to our spiritual life. One's religious choice is a personal decision. I do not judge anyone based on religion, atheism, or any belief system. I do not know, but I suspect You may care more for a person's actions, love, and charity than for their religious beliefs.

For me, I choose Christ. I believe that the life of Jesus of Nazareth was special, had special meaning, and His story is our story. It is a story that I choose as my meaning and my life.

I kneel and quiver before your awesome power and majesty, and I rest all my hope in You.

May Your will be done.

Amen.

Distilled Ancient Wisdom

The meaning of Jesus' life is that there is meaning to life.

There was a family in Galilee who were of royal and priestly genealogy, dedicated for generations to follow the Torah, and to raise up prophets and spiritual leaders. They produced such leaders as John the Baptist and James, the brother of Jesus, who practiced asceticism, humility, and spirituality. Jesus was raised in an environment supporting the learning of the Jewish scriptures and religion.

Jesus upheld the Jewish law in its totality, but he emphasized the inner spiritual meaning over the letter of the law. He taught that the Law was made for Man, not Man for the Law. As the core of His teaching, he taught the Law of Love; that is, the greatest law is to love God with all one's heart, all one's mind, and all one's soul; and secondly to love one's neighbor as oneself.

The first law is to love God with all one's heart, mind, and soul. But what do we mean by "love God"? What does it mean to love a spirit: an abstraction we can't see, hear, or touch? It seems clear we do not know exactly what God is and may not be able to agree on a definition. Perhaps the broadest possible definition of God is "the core purpose, meaning, and values behind the universe." By recognizing this higher reality—a true Purpose to existence and a reason to strive for good—a person is given the antidote to nihilism. Life is not pure happenstance without meaning, and one must strive for the good, the true, and the beautiful. This is the reason for human existence and for the existence of the universe, and we should cherish it.

The second law, to love one's neighbor as oneself, is the epitome of how we should live in community. Happiness is only found by loving others, helping others, and doing good work for others. No amount of material success can substitute for a loving community of people. What good is it to gain the whole world if one loses one's own soul?

Together, these two related laws of love summarize what Jesus taught, which is a Way of Being; a radical, selfless way of making life worthwhile. This Way of Being found fertile soil in the poor in spirit, the meek people of his time, and ever since. The law of love is more important than rituals and theology.

Indeed, Jesus' law of love gives meaning and purpose not only to humans but to animals and the whole universe. He said that a human life is worth many sparrows, thus implying that even a sparrow has worth and dignity. So has my dog, all animals, and even inanimate objects.

The meaning of Jesus' life is that life has meaning. Even though he lived only a very short life, was tortured to death, wrote no book, and ruled no country, His life still had and has meaning. His words and actions pointed to the inherent dignity and value of each human life. He lived, taught and associated with all the people, poor and despised included. He valued his friends and associates, the animals and plants he encountered, and lived his principles to the very end. His life was his message and his meaning. He won the war after losing every battle.

The meaning of Jesus' life is that there is meaning to life.

Son of God

Jesus was God's son, but God deserted him on the cross

Jesus was God's son, but he had to carry his own cross

Jesus expected the Day of the Lord and the Second Coming

To occur within one generation of his crucifixion

But it didn't

Jesus was God's son, but his legacy has been used to inspire,
instigate, and justify hatred, murder, war and torture

Jesus was God's son,

But he, like us, is hanging in the Balance
of a mysterious unknown Reality.

O Spirit of Mankind

When all is said and done, I still believe

Christ will endure

An ultimate symbol of the human condition.

He dreamed, he lived, he sacrificed

He was crucified and died.

By the power of his vision and his imagination, he rose again.

But like us all, he bore (and must bear) the weight
of unintended consequences.

Were he to set foot today in St. Peter's Cathedral

What would he think?

Of gigantic statues, gargantuan spaces,
and untold riches and wealth?

Of pomp and circumstance, of Popes and cardinals?

Through a Glass Darkly

O Lord my God, I beseech thee to forgive me.

I believe in you and your power to enlighten, to help, and to heal. You have all power to grant anything that is consistent with Your will.

But I have always wondered why belief is so important. Why not just tell us and show us exactly what is true and what you want without question or doubt? Could You not, in Your omnipotence, show us proof of the truth? Why make it so important a factor that we can believe things that are not self-evident? Is such an ability to believe even more important than love, charity, and ethical behavior?

But, yet again, I know that Jesus emphasized the importance of belief and faith, so it is very important, but why?

It is as if God, the pre-existent, all-powerful, all-knowing One, in creating all that is, so emptied Itself into the creative process that S/He, perhaps in an effort to transcend even Itself, partially broke a few things, or left them uncompleted, or perhaps had to temporarily practice self-restraint. Maybe S/He, in some sense, sacrificed Their preexistent Self in order to create such a transcendent and potent creation, in the faith and knowledge and belief that S/He would be fully re-constituted in the post-existence of all that is.

Or more likely, maybe S/He just knows that we are better off without full knowledge of all secrets, because such knowledge would prevent us from doing important things, or that we needed to be in partial ignorance in order to experience important things, or to flex our belief and faith for reasons beyond our understanding.

Maybe S/He is even giving us the chance to cooperate in bringing about some things? Maybe S/He is showing some faith and belief that we will ultimately do the right things?

After all, we humans must have faith in order to even get up out of bed each morning, knowing that we will die, that we will possibly face horrible suffering, and that for sure some humans have and will face horrible suffering. We must have a great faith to keep on trying without clear evidence that right prevails, that anything has any purpose, that there is any meaning at all to our existence. We, more than any other living thing we know of, must have faith and optimistic hope in the face of the unknown and the terrible, just in order to live our lives and keep on keeping on.

Therefore, I believe that there are reasons, purposes, and rewards for faith, and that all things will be righted in the end, made straight, and justified; that every tear will be wiped away, all living things will be rewarded appropriately, and everyone will be filled with joy.

Jesus Didn't Write a Book

Jesus didn't write a book.

If He had written a book, we would be debating every word, disputing every sentence, and arguing over the minutia of what it all means. A book written by Jesus, even though written in the human language of a particular time and place, would be idolized by us. How to translate a 2000-year-old document written in a 2000-year-old dialect into our current imperfect and inexact languages?

Instead, we have the four gospels and the letters of Paul and others. These documents give us nuanced insights into the life and teachings of Jesus, from different points of view, without carrying the weight of being The Book that He Wrote.

Jesus imparted His message via transformative experiences with his apostles. Then, each of them passed on the experience person-to-person to many others, who in turn passed it on down through the years to an exponentially growing number of people.

Written words are not enough to shock us out of our conditioned selves. On the road to Damascus, only an encounter with the Logos can inspire us to do the right things for the right reasons.

The meaning and the message of Jesus carrying His cross will outlast all written books and will never fade into nothingness.

Theodicy

Who, or what, is God?

We cannot know precisely, because God is infinite and beyond our understanding. God is the Omega Point, the asymptote approached by an exponentially increasing function of Purpose, Meaning, and Reason.

Our minds can't comprehend God, but we can gradually climb the curve of improving notions about God's attributes, and we have been so climbing the curve for thousands of years. For example, the Jewish peoples' early anthropomorphic ideas about God were honed through hundreds of years as prophets gradually saw that charity, love, and good behavior were more important than ritual. Then, Jesus continued this ascent by emphasizing the law of love, saying that love of God and love of one's fellow humans were at the core of the law.

So, in some sense, God is about love. The first part of the law of love is to love God with all one's heart, with all one's mind and with all one's soul, to put God at the head and top of all hierarchies. Humans are inherently hierarchical, and it is much better that we worship a transcendent God than to worship ourselves, another human being, an organization, a tribe, or a nation-state.

So God is about love. Then why so much suffering and evil in Their creation, and why do bad things happen to good people? Why do children die of cancer and other horrible diseases, why do natural disasters kill thousands of people, why the Holocaust? It is clear that God allows evil to exist in the universe S/He created.

Let us go back to the beginning. God is love, and so God desires other beings to love. God begat Their son, and the Holy Spirit emanated forth from them and they became a loving Trinity. Then God created the angels, pure spirits that God created from whole cloth, from scratch, in their final form. They did not evolve to become what they are. And this was good, even though some of them rebelled.

But God conceived of another kind of being and so created an evolving, lawful universe that would evolve stars, galaxies and eventually life and human beings. There were important characteristics that couldn't be created ex nihilo, but that had to evolve in a contingent universe. This evolving creation required some evil in the mix, in order to evolve as God desired and to create such complex life forms as humans. Yes, God could have created "humans" from scratch, like S/He did the angels, but those humans would have been different than we are. God judged that beings forged in the fire of self-determination, involving tough decisions, ultimate risks, sufferings, and trials, would have superior qualities, and in the end, be worth the costs.

God created us such that we would be more richly rewarded by helping to find our own way, by working hard to help create the good, the true, and the beautiful, and by learning to value hard, creative work towards meaningful goals.

God, being just and supremely loving the created beings, agonized over the costs and rewards, and determined that S/He should share in this created, contingent world and its sufferings. How could God expose created beings to such suffering if God were not willing to expose Itself as well? So, God decided that S/He should also suffer, in the form of Their only begotten Son, and that the sufferings of God, God's Son, and of people were all worth the costs.

Maybe God knew, before creating the world, that S/He would ultimately create a better world and better humans by being willing to sacrifice and suffer alongside humanity, and that humanity could attain a better state through some sacrifice and suffering than if they were placed in an ideal, pain free world right from the beginning. Maybe God could have created a world with absolutely no evil and no suffering but foresaw that an even greater world could be created through some suffering and sacrifice. Maybe a propensity to suffer and sacrifice in order to create transcendent value is a core attribute of God.

Perhaps God sacrificed God, in whole or in part, for the benefit of the creatures S/He was creating. Specifically, S/He may have, for reasons unknown to us, decided to sacrifice the ability to continually intervene in the created world to stop bad things from happening. In other words, S/He may have needed to give up absolute ongoing omnipotence. God could still influence creation, not only by setting of the initial conditions, but also through the Holy Spirit, and by the Incarnation of the only begotten Son, the Perfect human being, Jesus

Christ. This may help explain the existence of evil in a world created by a good God. Maybe, God even desires help from creatures in completing the evolving creation, and maybe even in re-creating the effective omnipotence of God.

We don't fully understand yet why suffering is necessary. But God is love, and sometimes the best love is tough love. And sometimes, tough love requires suffering, but the suffering cannot be compared to the glory that is to be.

Maybe God, Itself, sacrificed Itself, for Us.

Alien Beings

We are all aliens now.

Modern science teaches us that we are the products of blind, meaningless chance, and that given the immensity of the universe, there are probably other intelligent life forms, including in all probability many that are much more advanced than we are. Any day now, we may find evidence of such beings and come into close contact with them. If we encounter alien beings who are much more advanced and intelligent than we are, making us appear to them as ants appear to us, they may view all of our doings, traditions, thinking, and spirituality as meaningless and worthless. What happens if we contact advanced alien beings with a civilization far more advanced than our own and with alien beings who are far more intelligent than us? What if the aliens turn out to be not only atheists, but to view our religions as primitive superstitions, not worthy of serious consideration?

Well, even ants have sensibilities. I assert that this scenario would make it more important, even all important, that a Higher Power, a God Who loves human beings, exists and that we worship that God. I assert that this should in no way diminish the truth or value of our religions and our spiritual history. Religious belief is not only a function of intelligence, but rather a function of our lived spiritual histories as individuals, civilizations, and as a species. Our spiritual traditions and beliefs would still be just as valid and powerful, despite the beliefs and philosophies of other species and civilizations. In particular, the meaning of Jesus to Christians would still be valid, true, and powerful. We believe in an all-powerful God, and that God is much more powerful than any alien civilization.

But for that matter, what about the spiritual sensibilities and realities of the intelligent alien beings on our own planet, the other intelligent species here on earth? We don't know about their inner realities either, and they may have beliefs we can't understand. Even if they are not as intelligent as humans, at least in some ways, that does not mean their realities are not valid. What about the spiritual realities of whales and dolphins, crows, and parrots, octopuses and cuttlefish? I would not be surprised if they have beautiful understandings or intimations of the meaning of life and death, even if we may never have any way to learn about them.

But when you get right down to it, we are all alien beings, all of us including every human being. We each live in our own consciousness and can't really know what's going on in other humans' inner spiritual realities. We are strangers in a strange land, and we each have our own inner spirit and soul that we are responsible for. And we must each ultimately decide where we stand spiritually. We know that our God is bigger than any contingent being's religion, concepts, ideas, or beliefs, including any other alien beings, no matter how intelligent and advanced those beings might be.

And, our great God is the source of our hope. Being a God of sacrifice, we know S/He sacrificed Their only begotten Son for our sakes. And we know that our human lives require sacrifice and hardships, but they are made meaningful by Their sacrifice. Being greater than any evil, we know Their power and plan will ultimately make all sacrifice, all hardship, and all evil be worth the cost, and the end result will be the ultimate good. So, while we are strangers in a strange land, we are bound for glory in a home prepared for us by God, and all creatures, high and low, great and small, alien and common, will be brought into their proper home by an all-powerful God.

"All shall be well, and all shall be well, and all manner of thing shall be well." —Julian of Norwich

Ars Genetica

It seems that we are on the verge of a revolution in genetic engineering. It is now possible to alter DNA, including human DNA. Thus, I am confounded by the thought that future humans will be much more intelligent than I am, and better in every other way, also. Which brings up the question, what do we know about DNA?

DNA is extremely complex, and we know of no life that does not contain DNA. Presumably, it came into being at almost the same time as life on earth began. The primary known function of DNA is to code for proteins. Proteins themselves are fabulously complex, not only in their chemical formulae and bonds, but also in how they fold into convoluted shapes. The shapes of proteins are essential to their function, as they use a sort of "lock-and-key" mechanism to latch onto other proteins to do their work. All of this is astounding and if it were the only function of DNA (as was originally assumed) it would be wondrous indeed.

But only some of DNA codes for proteins, and the rest has always been called junk DNA. Curiously, the more complex a species, the higher the percentage of junk its DNA contains. Human DNA is said to be 98% junk, while simple bacteria DNA contains only 2% junk. Given how much we don't know, all these numbers are subject to change.

More recently, it has been discovered that some junk DNA does have a function, which is to act as a sort of on-off switching mechanism to guide the development of developing embryos. To me, this is just as amazing as coding to synthesize proteins, because the DNA is telling the developing embryo when and where to develop brain cells, bone cells, or other kinds of cells, and how to put it all together and configure a human being, or other life form.

But that still leaves more than 50% of human DNA as useless "junk". The word "hubris" comes to mind, so I propose another hypothesis.

What if this truly dark DNA is preprogrammed to guide evolution? What if this dark DNA acts to switch on selected evolutionary advances at appropriate times and places? Perhaps junk DNA contains information that will be needed in the future to develop new organs, body plans, and functions. And perhaps this junk DNA guides developing embryos on when and where to change, mutate, or modify their behavior. Sounds fantastic. But DNA IS fantastic. We don't know completely how major evolutionary developments happen, but maybe junk DNA has something to do with it.

The Unknown God

We are seeking, trying to find, or even to help re-create in full the reign of that God, the all-powerful, all-knowing, all good God Who will wipe away every tear, banish all evil, and establish justice.

We need and deserve that God.

And God will be what God will be.

Trust

Trust is an old Germanic word with no trace of Latin or Greek. Trust is practical, proactive, and leads to results.

Trust stands catercorner in the angle formed by faith and belief.

Faith is blind, belief is fickle, while trust is solid, warm, and alive, annealing the tension between faith and belief.

Where faith may fail, and belief may waver, trust is reliable, pragmatic, and sure.

Like with soldiers in battle, or teammates on the field, trust is a practical necessity. Trust is simple and pure.

Belief can be plagued with doubts, faith with fear, but trust is a habit that allows you to put one foot in front of another.

Belief is soft, faith fragile, trust hard.

Trust ain't no false prophet. Trust inspires action and fortitude, leading to deeds and accomplishments, and helps those who help themselves.

We trust each morning enough to get up and face life. Our society depends on trust for cooperation and economic activity.

The cells of our bodies trust each other to perform their jobs so that the whole organism can function properly.

God trusts people to help complete God's plans.

Jesus trusted Peter to lead his church, even though Peter was filled with contradictions, doubts, and fear. In order to avoid possible torture and death, Peter denied knowing Jesus in his hour of need. But Jesus trusted him anyway.

So let us tally up the trust of which we speak.

Trust is prosaic, quotidian, down to earth, and will see you through good times and bad, for better or worse, through life and death.

Trust means doing what's right, supporting the good, the true, and the beautiful. Even though you haven't got a clue how good will ultimately triumph over evil, you trust that it will.

Love means doing what's right, though you are not sure that good will triumph over evil.

Trust and love are related. Trust is love in action.

So trust in trust.

On Poetry

How can it be that words meld and merge into one another to create mellifluous phrases, that flow into sentient sentences, that cascade into an iridescent waterfall, reflecting and refracting semantic sunlight into an ecstatic prismatic dance?

The Tongues of Men
and of Angels

To begin by looking at the big picture, the one and only thing we know for certain is that we, as limited human beings, cannot be absolutely certain about anything. Science is a process of getting better and better answers to questions, but it can never obtain the end point of certainty, especially about matters of substance. The origins of things are lost in the mists of time.

Because of this uncertainty, it is possible that there is no meaning, no purpose, no God, no creator, and no values in the universe, which leads to nihilism. Radical materialism, scientism, and logical positivism paint an impoverished and dreary picture of our situation.

And even if we choose to believe that there is an omnipotent and omniscient creator God, then that God did not see fit to give us all the facts in an unambiguous, undeniable way. If that God is benevolent and in charge, then evidently a decision was made that we were better off not knowing what the detailed purpose and meanings behind existence are unless, or until, we could decipher and learn those things on our own. An omnipotent God could have given us instructions, answers, and let us know definitively that S/He existed and that our optimal happiness could be achieved by doing things in a certain way.

But one thing we do have is an inner mental life, an inner space that to us is perhaps more real in some ways than anything else. And even if our conscious inner life came about by random chance with no prior purpose or meaning at all, the closest thing we have to certainty is that this inner life exists and is real. We can interpret the meaning and value of this inner life. It seems to have value and meaning for a time, even if it is temporary. And we don't really know anything about time and what it really is anyway, so our current moments of existence are what are accessible to us and seem to be important to us.

And our inner selves can perceive beauty. Although there is ugliness, there is also beauty: the beauty of the natural world, love between humans, and the human-created beauty of art and religion. In fact, art and religion are efforts to communicate to the broad world the inner values and beauty that are perceived by an inner self. We can try to make the beauty outweigh the ugliness, to achieve an inner world that is at least a 51% good inner world for ourselves, and to share it with the broader world, if we so choose. One thing of beauty we can cherish is language. This little book is an attempt by me to explore the beauty of language. Language is an interesting phenomenon and can be quite beautiful. Before language was invented and developed, it would have been impossible to imagine it. And language was created by human beings, so we can say for sure that a thing of beauty and value has been created, and it was created by us. None of us created language all by ourselves, but collectively we have made it what it is today. We are all still contributing to it. Imagine ten thousand generations of mothers teaching their children to talk, teaching language itself to generations of children. It is difficult to imagine anything more noble.

And while we cannot point to anything that is certain, even by using language, logic, and mathematics, we can—by using language—invent and describe an infinity of possible certainties. Which is astounding, if you think about it.

Now, having created language, a thing that couldn't have been talked about, envisioned, or predicted prior to its creation, how can we be sure that people will not in the future create something that we presently cannot imagine, predict, or even conceptualize, that will be of greater value, interest, and beauty than language, perhaps of much greater value and beauty?

So, having created language, a thing of astonishment, wonder, and beauty, what might we create next, and how beautiful and interesting might that be?

Could it be a new form of consciousness, as far ahead and beyond our current consciousness as language is beyond whatever form of inner mental world was in the heads of our human ancestors before they created language? We know our brains have a great deal of plasticity; they can be reconfigured by necessity and environmental circumstances, and even by taking thought and effort. For instance, when the brain is injured and portions of it are completely disabled, the functions previously performed by that part of the brain can be gradually assumed and performed by another, previously unrelated part of the brain. Or a person who practices a particular skill intensely for a long time, such as playing the piano, can cause the portion of the brain involved to grow and enlarge itself. Taxicab drivers in London have larger cerebrums than other people, on average, and larger cerebrums than they had before learning "the Knowledge" of how to navigate London's streets without the aid of GPS. How great, novel, and beautiful might a new higher form of consciousness be? We cannot even imagine it, just as pre-language humans could not imagine language.

And to aid and abet an enhanced consciousness, might we invent a new and enhanced form of language, combining alphabetic script with color-coded, iconic, multimedia hieroglyphics, Chinese characters, and emojis? Or, more likely, something beyond anything I can even imagine?

There is room for more creation.

玄 言 :-)

Time out of Mind

Time is God's first and foremost invention, for without time there would be no change, and without change there would be no life. This central trinity: time, change, and life, begat the growth of novelty. Only God could figure out how to create something beyond eternal perfection, even if that creation involves struggle and suffering. Time begets life and death, for all life lives in time, and all life dies in time. Good and bad, yin and yang, life and death allow for growth, creation, and novelty. But death has a sting. When a person dies, they are often completely forgotten, as if that person had never lived. A human life has a duration, and then we perceive it to be completely gone. This annihilation stings, and we wonder if it is worthwhile.

But there is another perspective on time. Since we don't really know what time is, could the duration of a human life, or anything else that happens in time, have an intrinsic value that we don't understand, and a meaning that transcends our everyday perception of time? Certainly, everything that happens affects everything else, and any human life has connections and causes other things to happen, creating a cascading effect on the rest of reality that never goes away.

Quantum physics hypothesizes that at the smallest scales, time itself is really the relationship between and amongst causes and effects; that is, when particles and energy fields interact, time is the resulting ordering of outcomes. In other words, without events, causes, and effects, there would be no time. Time without events is meaningless. Words can't do justice to this subject, but there is something about time that leaves a door open for meanings beyond our normal perspectives. Certainly, time allows for the novelty of creation and evolution of great things. Shouldn't there be a destiny, a purpose, and a meaning to each human life beyond its end point at death?

For instance, what about my ancestors. Ordinary though they were, what about Dr. John Stephens of Gloucester (1589-1675) who emigrated to Virginia in 1634. Without him, my Stephens family in America would not have existed. Or what about his descendant, Revolutionary War veteran Moses Stephens, who migrated to Kentucky after the war and raised a large family of daughters and sons. And then what about Civil War Union soldier Louis Stephens of Kentucky, and my grandfather Sherman Stephens, a WWI veteran who helped liberate Paris? My father, Kenneth Stephens, married Wilma Vanover, and the Vanover family also had deep roots in southeastern Kentucky. The Vanover family helped found Indian Creek Baptist Church in a cave in McCreary County Kentucky. I attended the simple white church house that succeeded the cave, and loved the God-fearing ladies who cooked and brought the fried chicken, dumplings, and pies to the church picnics. My maternal grandmother, Elsie Vanover (nee Crabtree) was as good, gregarious, wholesome, and lovable a person as ever lived. What about all of them; do their lives count for nothing now that they are gone or is there more to this than meets the eye?

On the other extreme, consider the person Jesus of Nazareth. By any standard, He is still influencing more people than perhaps any other person. He took the Jewish ideas of people being created in the image of God, and therefore the infinite worth of every human, and spread it worldwide. Surely His life is interconnected with everything today, and to a lesser extent, so are the lives of every human who has ever lived. And even after He lived and died...

Something happened...

An empty tomb was found...

What it meant, who knew? But after the women found the empty tomb, His disciples kept seeing Him in appearances of various kinds. An empty tomb, appearances, not of a Zombie, not of a resuscitated corpse, but of a victorious glorified person in a glorified body. His followers saw that something happened, and they went from utter despair and depression to joyful confidence and exuberance. They didn't know what had happened, but they knew something had happened. It didn't make sense, but then maybe it did. Something had happened, and although we may never know exactly what or how, it mattered; it matters, and it will always matter. When something happens, it makes a difference and this was, and is, the extreme example.

Consider my younger sister, Amy Stephens. A sweeter, kinder, gentler, and more worthwhile person never lived. She was born 20 weeks premature and at less than two pounds, had to have critical surgery to remove one of her malformed lungs. It was more than six months before she finally got out of the hospital. Then, because of her small size and weight, and a less than robust lung, she was in and out of the hospital several times as an infant for various serious infections.

Always on the small size, she was a bit fragile, but she was fun-loving and loved horses and all animals. Everyone loved her. She was always there to console me when I was down as a teenager and in my twenties. She had a knack for knowing when she could help me just by being there and talking and walking with her older brother. She was beloved by her family, her schoolmates, and by the congregation of the small Afton Baptist Church. As we drove to the church on Sunday mornings, we often stopped to pick up an elderly gentleman who waited on the side of the road, to take him to church with us. He seemed to us to be 100 years old. He especially loved Amy. On his birthday every year, he always sang solo and acapella, the old African American spiritual "Just a Closer Walk with Thee". He could barely mouth the words, and his voice was so weak that he could hardly be heard. One wondered whether he could finish the song each year, but he always did, stumbling along to the bitter end no matter what. It was as moving and magnificent as Pavarotti or Caruso.

> I am weak but Thou art strong
> Jesus keep me from all wrong
> I'll be satisfied as long
> As I walk, let me walk close to Thee
>
> Just a closer walk with Thee
> Grant it, Jesus, is my plea
> Daily walking close to Thee
> Let it be, dear Lord, let it be
>
> When my feeble life is o'er
> Time for me will be no more
> Guide me gently, safely o'er
> To Thy kingdom's shore, to Thy shore

Just a closer walk with Thee
Grant it, Jesus, is my plea
Daily walking close to Thee
Let it be, dear Lord, let it be

Did this man's life matter, does it still matter? How about my little sister, Amy? Amy, oh my Amy, how could it be, how could it happen? At the age of 17, just as her life was coming into focus, it was Christmas season and she had her first paying job, as a nurse's aide in an old folks' home. Those seniors loved her, and she sure loved them, she was doing good; her life had more meaning, her problems were fading. For the first time in her life, she had enough of her own money to go out and buy Christmas presents for each family member, with her own hard-earned money. She was out shopping and on her way home, but running a bit late, with a little snow and ice on the road, and she skidded off the highway just a quarter mile from our driveway. As she veered into a neighbor's yard, she must have seen the fence pole heading for her windshield; surely she could avoid, re-do, or somehow correct the error, the horrible situation of the moment, the awful still-framed frozen moment, and then it rammed right through the glass and right into her skull, Oh no! How could it be? How could she endure; how could this happen? Amy, I didn't believe it. Even when I visited the hospital and saw your swollen head I could not accept it and refused to believe it. How could God let this happen; how could it happen? Oh Amy, my angel.

My Dad heard the accident and was the first on the scene to see the obscene wooden fence post rammed through her brain. His baby girl, his pride and joy, his angel. My parents were never the same, ever. It was senseless, beyond belief or understanding. After she died, my dad paid the hospital bills and totaled up the insurance payment to discover insurance had paid for everything except $1.01. Which he somehow recalled was the amount the insurance company had over-paid when Amy was in the hospital as a newborn infant, through all her medical trials, $1.01. The next-door neighbor made a big deal out of needing reimbursement for his damaged fence. The books were balanced here on earth but not in heaven.

What is, was, and will be the balance of Amy's life? It's not just a mechanical record of 17 years. I recall Brother Jones at Afton Baptist Church, preaching from the pulpit in full sweat, saying "I have been to the mountaintop, I hear the music of heaven and I know my Re-deemer liveth. He will dry every tear and right every wrong, we will be reunited at the river, over Jordan, just a closer walk with thee." Jesus offered peace and love to everyone, He taught the Sermon on the Mount, blessed are the poor, the peacemakers, the humble. He willingly went to the cross to offer His life for His friends, He asked his Father to forgive those who crucified Him, He forgave the thief on the cross, He didn't say you had to be Catholic, or Protestant, or Jewish, He gave His forgiveness and His sacrifice for everyone. He didn't say you had to have just the right dogma or theology or beliefs, you just had to love God and your neighbor, and trust in Him. He wasn't prejudiced against Hindus, Buddhists, or future Muslims...He did tell us to love one another, turn the other cheek and love our ene-mies. Huh? Hard to fathom...He did say our righteousness needed to exceed that of the Pharisees and other clerics of His day...no respecter of rich or powerful people...blessed are the poor. He loved. I have seen the light, hallelujah, and I've seen the first and the last, the resurrec-tion of the lamb. That's all, Hallelujah. I put all my hope in Him.

And if I get on the wrong side of some debate, some ideology, some formula, or some belief, one thing I am certain of...

Wherever I am welcome is where I'll be.

History and Destiny
of the Human Heart

What's so special about human beings, given that we can now make machines that outdo us in many kinds of intelligence, and now that many scientists think there is no meaning to anything? Is there any significance to humanity beyond the tenets of extreme scientific materialism?

Well, for one thing, we have depth. Billions of years of evolution, starting with physical and chemical evolution, but let's focus on biological evolution. Beginning with the first living cell, there is complexity beyond anything we can currently make. Looking under a microscope, one can see that the simplest of living cells has mobility, willpower, life, and spirit. It seeks food and flees danger. It struggles to survive, and it reproduces. The DNA it contains is complex beyond anything we can even imagine creating.

Multicellular animals take this to a new level. How does the DNA in a cell know how to divide, subdivide, differentiate, and organize into a complex cellular being? Even on a strictly scientific materialist level, this is unfathomable. But in the biosphere of earth, all the variety and complexity are built on individual cells. And each cell is itself still a unique living being. In a human being, each of our trillions of cells is alive. Each cell is differentiated and plays a perfect role in its organ, and each organ plays its role in the complete human being. But in addition, each cell has its own life, its drive, its will, its spirit.

In the future, one can foresee that humans will increasingly become parts of much larger, ever more complex systems. These systems will be comprised of many human beings, with each human being specialized in its contribution to the overall society. We are social animals like ants and bees, but much more sophisticated. Our future evolving civilizations will include technology, machinery, computers, software, and artificial intelligence of great power. But it is critical that we maintain the identity, value, and spiritual awareness of each individual human.

The core essential attribute of each human is spiritual. Every society known has always had a spiritual and religious reality. Religions have a societal role of great importance, and the origin and source are always individual human spiritual experience. Human spiritual experience cannot be expressed completely in mere words. But in each age and in every civilization, prophets have arisen who are especially spiritually astute and uniquely able to communicate and educate their societies. It is probable that these prophets were often, perhaps usually, women, but due to human culture it is the male prophets who were documented historically. But in any case, these prophets always had the same core spiritual message, although they also had to express their message in terms that their culture could understand. This resulted in dogmas appropriate to each culture and time. But we should realize that these dogmas are decorations, important and beautiful decorations, but still decorations around the core spiritual experiences. We must not let the various dogmas with which the prophets exhorted and explained their revelations to their societies divide us in this day and age.

We should focus on the spiritual essence of each prophet's message, which is always the same.

We are privileged to have access to so many beautiful spiritual traditions, and each has unique and surpassing beauty. We can cherish the core spiritual essence of all these traditions, while practicing our own traditions, rituals, and cultures, and affirming and enjoying the beauty of all the world's spiritual streams.

And we can see that, over the long term, human religions have evolved favorably, and have gotten better in the sense of gradually eliminating negative characteristics and highlighting ethics, moralism, and pluralism. For instance, we no longer practice human sacrifice, and our Gods are now global rather than tribal.

Each prophet had a profound spiritual experience and used its insights to help educate humanity. But it is obvious that the religions they founded and the scriptures they wrote are in no way infallible. Nothing associated with human beings can ever be infallible, and the various dogmas are shown to be, in their literal details, incorrect in some ways, while the spiritual core can still be valid. We must not fight and argue over the details of dogma.

Given the immense complexity of human cultural history, I make no apology for summarizing the story of the prophets even though some will complain that I am leaving out much of importance. I do especially regret not including the many women whom I am certain contributed more than their fair share to our religious heritage, but our cultures just did not document them. Be that as it may, I herein survey our entire spiritual history from eight miles high and a bird's-eye view.

At some point, evolving humans began to conceptualize cause and effect, discern the idea of spiritual powers behind our world, and to conceive of the idea of divinity. It was at this point that we use Adam and Eve to symbolize those first prophets who announced and expounded their spiritual experiences of God.

Later, perhaps around 2000 B.C., Abraham refined some of the religious insights of the Mesopotamian, the Egyptian, and the Canaanite religions into a synthesis to honor the high God named El in the Semitic tongues. Abraham removed some older practices such as child sacrifice and began the journey to a more transcendental idea of God and a monotheistic religion.

Later still, Zarathustra, or Zoroaster, depending on your linguistic transcription preference, took the raw material of the Indo-European peoples of Persia and purified them by removing some outmoded practices and the multitude of gods and refined and focused them to a more dualist conception emphasizing a battle between Good and Evil, Light and Darkness, and came up with a more spiritual and ethical religion that later influenced Judaism, Christianity and Islam.

Then, back in the Semitic world, Moses took the Abrahamic traditions and combined them with Egyptian and local desert influences of the God named Yahweh, and took the religion even more in a monotheistic direction, and coded a set of ethical laws including the Ten Commandments modeled on the laws of Hammurabi. Moses' laws were a milestone in ethical religion.

Next, between around 800 and 300 BC, a period of great spiritual deepening occurred all over the Old World, known as the axial age.

In China, Confucius (author of the *Analects*), Laozi (author of the *Tao Te Ching*), and Zhuang Zhou (don't miss his book *Zhuangzi*), took traditional Chinese folk religion and ancestor worship and created ethical Confucianism and spiritual Taoism.

In India, the polytheistic and philosophical Hindu traditions were transformed into Buddhism by Gautama Buddha and into Jainism by Mahavira. They eliminated practices such as the caste system and emphasized ethical philosophy.

In the Middle East, a whole host of Israeli prophets emphasized the ethics and the superiority of the spirit over ritual purity.

In Greece, Pythagoras, Plato, Aristotle, and many others went beyond the Indo-European polytheistic systems to recognize a logical and ethical Supreme Being over all.

The axial age was a remarkable synchronistic happening in which most of the native religions of the Old World were transformed into second-level versions that are superior in some important ways. The fact that they occurred in so many places and cultures at roughly the same time implies that they represented a logical and reasonable development in human affairs.

After the axial age, the hinge of history was Jesus Christ who took the evolving Judaic religion and, while completely honoring the ancient religious traditions, in line with the spiritual directions of the axial age Hebrew prophets, He took it to a more universal spiritual conclusion, emphasizing even more the importance of the spirit, ethics, and love over ritual purity and mere legal codes. He preached on the arch-importance of love for God and love for all our fellow beings. The Sermon on the Mount is the pinnacle of spiritual discourse.

This was followed in the Middle East by Muhammad who re-emphasized monotheism and who recognized spiritual evolution from a common source for many of the Middle Eastern religious traditions. He was original in promoting religious commonality.

More recently, the Baha'i Faith was born in nineteenth century Persia and its founder Baha'u'llah continued and extended the recognition of the common source and evolution of religion through all the major prophets and religious traditions in history around the world. Universal Unitarianism in the West also recognized the commonality in all major religions without prejudice.

At the time, each of the prophets preached their religious truths. They based them on core religious experiences, but they also decorated them with rituals, myths, and stories to try to explain reality. These various diverging mythologies have sometimes divided the peoples of the world and many of the stories and decorations are no longer acceptable or needed. But the core spiritual experiences are still valid and are being repeated even today. We must not let the different details of each historical religion divide us. If we are to disagree and fight and hate over religious differences, we would be better off with no religions at all. But we need religions to express core spiritual realities of humanity.

We need to find a Middle Way, in which we cherish our spiritual traditions and build a better world based on love and recognition of our common spiritual heritage and nature. We need to nurture our spirituality, while at the same time working hard to build a better world. We can't fight over narrow definitions of religion, but our brains are hard-wired for spiritual and religious belief. If we don't worship an ultimate rational Power, then we will worship something far worse.

The future will be different, complex, and challenging. But we must always return to the inner spiritual reality of our situation. We are spiritual beings on our way home. The material civilizations we create are also important and we value them, but we must not worship them, despite their ever-increasing power.

If one hypothesizes that Mind precedes Matter, and that Mind is primary and came first, then one can contemplate that God, the primeval and original Conscious Mind, sent forth pieces of conscious mind that have eventually evolved into us. We have the conscious ability to exercise some of God's attributes. Each of us contains a conscious core of awareness. But how can we ever know that God exists, or that God truly loves us? We can't, unless we become once again a part of the Mind of God.

What is the destiny of the human heart? To be reunited with God, from whom we are apart. Maybe that's why God sent us out in the first place, so we could all come back and share our stories together as part of one Mind.

In the meantime, we can occupy ourselves with moving towards the Omega Point of history, while drinking spiritual nourishment from the living waters deep within us, and by valuing (but not worshipping!) the hard work of our human hands as we build the foundations for New Jerusalem.

Time Revisited

Heavenly time is different from our normal time. This can be visualized using the image of a cross, with heavenly time running along the horizontal crossbeam, and our normal time running vertically down the main post, orthogonal to the crossbeam. From the perspective of heavenly time, our normal time is all visible: past, present, and future. The Godhead is symbolized by a circle or a sphere on top of the cross and is infinite beyond all space and time, beyond words, and beyond the capacity of any religion to comprehend or express. We are created in the image of the Godhead and Its emanation into the cross of heaven and earth. But of course, we fall so short of the goal that we sometimes resemble Zombies more than fully conscious creatures. Nonetheless the potential is there. But it is contingent upon a struggle between good and evil and requires our participation.

The vertical time flow of which we are a part inherently introduces change of two types. First, there is entropy, which is the random tendency to disorder. Because our universe obeys natural law, it introduces the existence of natural evil. This natural evil includes such things as death, cancer, tsunamis, as opposed to willful evil that may be executed by beings such as ourselves. Natural evil, as well as willful evil, involves a great deal of suffering. It is apparent that an all-good, all-powerful, and all-knowing God would not have chosen to create time, with its inherent natural evil, unless it also created a greater good.

That greater good may be the potential good fostered by conscious beings like ourselves in actively choosing, loving, and creating goodness, and opposing the forces of evil and entropy. We are fighting for the good and against the forces of evil, as in Zoroastrian theology. God rolled the die and is taking a big gamble on us. But being that God is God, I like the odds on our side.

Meanwhile, we, like Christ, are being crucified on a cross of time. There is no escaping the temporal suffering involved, but it is all for the greater glory that is to be.

Exit Interview

Thank you for granting me this chance to explain our point of view. You are obviously more intelligent and have access to more information and your civilization is far more advanced, and I realize we must seem trivially simple to you, and you may or may not see value in our continued existence. But let me give you some thoughts.

While each of us humans is limited to our individual sensory inputs, we do have shared stories, memories, conclusions and theories developed over many generations and hundreds and thousands of years.

Because the universe is so elaborate, we believe that it has some purpose, even though we don't know what that purpose is. We believe, given that the purpose is grander than we can imagine, it may include intelligence and reasons that are completely opaque to us. It might therefore be that this purpose could include logical reasons for what may seem to us to be absurdities of our existence and our reality.

It does seem to us absurd that complex thinking, conscious animals are each individually doomed to die. And of what value is their suffering? When you look at us, why should you be concerned if we, as a whole species and civilization, cease to exist? From your greatly higher position, knowledge, and point of view, you may ask why you should be any more concerned with our troubles and our existence or nonexistence as the universe apparently is. Maybe you should even step on us like we might step on an ant, or exterminate us as we might an ant colony.

We think your knowledge, opinions, and theories are of immense import and interest, but we also do not know that you are the ultimate reality or in touch with the ultimate purpose. There may be a higher level power that could still make and execute judgments beyond your knowledge and control. Who is to say whether information is conserved and never destroyed? Who is to say that the past does not exist? Who is to say that moral judgments beyond our kin will not be exercised? For these reasons we abide with a deep faith that all will be well in the end, and hope for outcomes unseen. We endure all hardships, seek equitable justice, and trust in providence. This is our point of view, and we honor it. It is better to have lived and died as an insignificant little creature than never to have lived at all.

But let me say just a little bit more. Our Reality is a large crystal. The crystal has an Absolute Apex that flows forth into the whole crystal in a volumetric explosion of colors, flowers, and shapes beyond our imagination, and contains many streaks of localized intensity and development. Each streak is a thread-like skein of even more internal connectedness, complexity, and inter-relatedness and each streak is also intimately connected with all the other streaks, in complex ways that co-determine intimate development. Our own streak is actually a timestream; we inhabit and experience our own now as a speck in this stream. We view our past as events closely connected to our speck, but behind it; and anticipate our future as close-by specks that are still in front of us. We do not see at all the myriad intimate connections between our stream and all the other streaks. These connections are completely invisible to us, but they control, constrain, and enhance the development of our stream.

Everything in the crystal is eternal in that the crystal is permanent and exists outside of what we call time. So, our speck, our current now, will always exist and has always existed as part of the crystal. Likewise, our past and our future have always existed and will always exist, although we cannot perceive that from our current speck of time. So, we take care with how we live each moment because we will have to live with these moments forever.

When God the Parent created the crystal, S/He created it in such a way that it would evolve in fabulous and elaborate ways that are beyond our understanding, and so as to bring ultimately favorable results including for us puny creatures, but in order to do this it involves some suffering and pain. We cannot possibly perceive why or how, because it involves the elaborate interconnections between the many streaks and throughout the crystal. When God's Son created our stream, He did so in accordance with all the Parent's plans and He created it to evolve in a timestream to begat creatures such as us. He incarnated at the appropriate place and time and He will return again at the end of our timestream. This timestream has the capability to encapsulate time in such a way as to ultimately create a capsule that will have a subjectively infinite and eternal amount of time. That is, our entire stream including the ending time capsule exists inside the crystal, but to creatures such as us, the amount of information processed per unit of our time will increase exponentially and to us as creatures it will seem to be an eternity. This is our paradise.

Consider the paradisiacal subjectively eternal time capsule at the end of our timestream. It will seem infinitely long to those living in it because each time period will incorporate infinitely more conscious experience and information content than the preceding time period. This will be engineered by the massive information computing power of the society of conscious beings led by Jesus, the Son of God, after His return. Everything good from preceding times will be resurrected there, nothing good will be wasted and nothing bad or evil will be allowed into the paradisiacal time capsule. Every person who ever lived will see all the good within them resurrected. But if a person is resurrected, which person will it be; the child, the young person, or the old person? There are an infinite number of persons in the many moments of our lives. Perhaps a composite will beresurrected. In addition, every good possibility springing from a good person or thing will be manifested in all its glory.

We may not know the details and the exactness because we are limited creatures of low understanding, and so our ideas are more metaphor and simile than fact, but the underlying meaning is there and is of value and we cherish what we collectively are imagining. You should see the value and honor it like we honor the value of crows and parrots, whales and dolphins, chimpanzees, gorillas and orangutans, and elephants and octopuses.

Value is value, and everything of value in the crystal is preserved.

The Parent is beyond our imaginings, and it scares us. A Fire that must completely dissolve and consume many things in order to create many things. The Son who created our timestream is more approachable and understands us better. We each wander about our stream as if it matters and it does matter to us. Some sense their fate and adhere to it and stay beautifully on the path, with each decision following the logic of their fate. Others go off-skein and make confused decisions, bouncing them from stem to stern amongst the many paths within the multiverse. Each one of us helps to unfold the infinitely branching multiverse of our timestream.

So, please consider taking us seriously. We have thoughts, ideas, and aspirations. We are very interested in your knowledge, theories, and opinions, which are based no doubt on superior data, knowledge, and cogitation; but please don't be surprised if we don't automatically just abandon our ideas when they conflict with yours. There may be more things than are dreamed of in your philosophy.

Lastly, the language of this message is very simple, and a poor vehicle for imparting the underlying thoughts, and the message itself may seem to you to be of little import. Nonetheless, if taken as a whole, it contains a spirit and a depth, and it is more than the sum of its parts, its words, sentences, and paragraphs.

Both the language and the message, simple though they may be, are the result of a long process of intuitive evolution, involving pain and suffering, as well as glory and transcendence, by a bottom-up process of a long-suffering society, a continual and on-going collective process of giving birth. They are not, nor could they be, the result of top-down deductive logic and mathematics. They are a participatory creation, not the result of a fiat creation, put into the mouth of a Zombie-like creature.

Long live the messiness of life.

Coda

The Zombie Thirsts

The big picture is this. There is a reason why we exist, why consciousness exists, but we don't know what that reason is. We feel like we are missing something important, but we don't know what. We are driven on a quest to find the missing substance to quench our thirst for meaning, but we find we are in a bit of a spiritual desert.

We are all, to some extent, Zombie-like and robotic. There are constant pressures in our society to Zombify us. We are conditioned to believe that everything is mechanistic, including life and ourselves. We are in awe of the advances science has made in helping us to understand how the universe works, and grateful for the advances of technology, but in terms of our outlook on life, our philosophy, and our hope for meaning, the pendulum is swinging towards scientism and nihilism.

In our search, language is woefully inadequate. I lament its inadequacy and ineptness. It is a crude tool that breaks, distorts, and maims attempts to express the deepest matters. Metaphor is the best we have, and that old compendium, compilation, and collection of books we call the Bible is a rich source of apt metaphors.

In the very first book of the old Hebrew Torah, the Spirit of God moves upon the waters. The waters of life feature prominently in the Prophets, Jesus offers living water to the Samaritan woman at the well, saying she will never again thirst after tasting it, and in the Book of Revelations the New Jerusalem features a fountain of living waters flowing deep and wide.

And we all do have one thing within each of us that goes beyond our conditioned, robotic behavior. If you look within, you will find a deep well of consciousness that no one can take away from you or deny. You can dip your bucket deep down in the well waters and pull up refreshment that is not merely mechanical, not reductive, not Zombie-like and not robotic. This deep well of consciousness is there within you, and you can access it at any time and believe in its reality and its significance.

If, despite all of the evil that you see in the world, you believe it possible that God's love could be an infinite ocean of living water capable of sustaining your consciousness forever... then you can quaff the elixir of the ages.

About the Author

Ronald Dean Stephens was born on October 19, 1952, in Cincinnati, Ohio. He received degrees in physics and mathematics from DePauw University and in Business Administration from the University of Cincinnati. He worked for more than 47 years in the electronics industry, including as president of three different companies designing and manufacturing crystal oscillators, precision timing devices that are essential to commercial and military space programs, including the GPS system. Ron and his wife Kathleen have four beautiful children, Meghan, Rebecca, Jennifer, and Michael. Ron has written poetry and prose continuously for over 50 years, exploring the meaning of life, and focused on his interests in philosophy, religion, and science. As a youth, Ron belonged to a Baptist church. Being interested in world religions, and studying them, he joined the Baha'i Faith for several years in his 40's and early 50's, before joining the Catholic Church at the age of 65. Ron has resided in Redondo Beach California for the last 17 years.

A Note on Chinese Character Radicals

Chinese characters have a history going back at least 4,000 years. They began as pictorial logographs and then evolved to include phonetic characteristics. Modern Chinese script is very complex but reflects the result of thousands of years of evolution.

One aspect of modern Chinese is the use of (approximately) 214 "radicals". Radicals are mostly very ancient logographs and are often used as root characters in modern Chinese words, often supplemented by additional characters that are phonographic in nature.

These radicals contain the depth of the ancient Chinese pictographs and thus a visual consonance and resonance not available from western written alphabetic scripts.

Alphabetic scripts have many obvious advantages, but the visual nature of Chinese characters are different and can be used to add depth to alphabetic writings, and furthermore, the same Chinese characters can be used unchanged with various different alphabetic scripts.

The minimal suggested usage of Chinese radicals hinted at in this book represent only one very simple such use, with the hope that much more meaningful ideas will be developed in the future.

After Poem

Every ending's a beginning
And every beginning's an ending.

So now, Adieu!

I must attend to very different chores.
But as I roam on distant shores
If you should come upon this little book
Pray pick it up and take a look.

Printed in the USA
CPSIA information can be obtained
at www.ICGtesting.com
CBHW072048090124
3197CB00001B/2